To my friend, Brenda
Jill Shearer

EASTBOUNDERS

Two Women Trucking
Through The Barriers

AUTHOR: JILL SHEARER

Copyright © 2010 JILL SHEARER
All rights reserved.
ISBN:13: 978 1460922217
ISBN-10: 1460922212

DEDICATION:

I would like to dedicate this book to my sister, Peggy Warmack and her husband David. She and her husband, put up with many phone calls at all times of the day and night. Their encouragement and support helped me to continue writing, when I was at my lowest. Thanks Peg and Dave,
From your big sister, Jill

ACKNOWLEDGMENTS & PREFACE

In 1973 I had a life changing experience. It was such a great change, and such a difficult change, and at the same time exciting and fun change, that I have always wanted to write about it, so other people could know what it was like for a woman to try working in an almost all male orientated and dominated job.

I thought a biography would be a good way to go. However, when I started writing, I found the rest of my life so normal and uninteresting, I knew I had to find another way to tell my story.

The next idea was to write a novel involved in building characters and having them travel through the episodes of my experiences. I thought this would loose its impact. The characters, being the dominant story, would diminish the experiences I was excited tell.

My experience was about myself and another woman, living United States. We actually quit our counseling and teaching jobs in 1973. We moved to California in a fifth wheel and attended truck driving school in Los Angeles. Our aim was to be able to drive a truck cross country as an occupation.

We both had a deep thirst to see the rest of the united States. So I'm back to a biography, only it will be a partial biography of a special time in my life. It is special because it was an unorthodox job, for women living in those days.

In developing this trip, I found I could work many of my episodes in. This would show how difficult it was, in 1973 for a woman to intrude into a male dominated occupation. I used the word (intrude) because the way some drivers treated us, made us feel like intruders. However many drivers were great and happy to see us out there on the road.

I made a list of the incidents I could remember. I read them off and they turned out to be either hysterical, or difficult, or both.

Most of them were in the first trip because we were unequipped to handle the job, even if we had completed trucking school.

In remembering these incidents, I could not always remember where they happened but I could remember them with details. The incidents were impressed on my mind, but not names of people or towns where they happened. Therefore, I decided to keep towns, roads, highways, mountains, people and companies private for their protection.

So this biography is a part of my life, which affected me so greatly, I didn't forget the main happenings over a thirty-seven year span. When you read this book you will see how exciting and educating these new experiences were.

I would like to thank the counselor of my school, for having an adventurous soul and spending this time with me, as the second half of the driving team.

Also I want to thank Peggy Warmack, my sister who constantly encouraged me to write on, when I was down and unsure about writing this. Also Colette Eisele, who read the first chapter and said this book, was surely worth continuing on and completing. Thanks to Barbe tanner for support on health problems. I thank Linda Bethane for my pictures.

Also thanks to Carolyn Krill for being a good friend. Kathy Mohar also read the first chapter and gave me encouragement to finish it. Flo Palumbo was always there for me.

Ann Milton was encouraging and knowledgeable about how to prepare this publishing. Since, I had never written a MS before, she graciously explained how to polish this MS for publishing. Without her help I probably wouldn't have been published. Chris Morningforest deserves thanks for my cover and much encouragement. So back to the MS, of my most life changing experiences. I took most of the experiences I could remember and put them in the first cross-country trip we made. I'm sure when you read for this book you will understand why these true incidents were imprinted on my mind forever.

As you have just read, my biography has been assembled in one special time. I wanted to share it with everyone. It is a time I wouldn't trade for anything.

Chapter 1

As I stepped down from the driver's seat of a huge Mac truck, I could feel the cool Los Angeles late evening air hit my warm body. I was completely soaked with perspiration, from driving this eighteen-wheeler on the freeway. I heard some chuckling to my left, and looking over that way I saw three members of my driving class standing in the shadows.

I started to answer, when I heard my instructor say, "Hey fellows, we just came back from Pomona."

"She can't drive on the freeway," they yelled out and laughed.

"Oh yes she can and did," Joe responded.

The driving students wondered off as Joe and I walked towards the classroom. When we reached the room he closed the door behind me.

"You stretched that story a bit, Joe," I said.

"They had it coming." He said with a smile on his face. He critiqued my first freeway trip. It was worth my sweaty body to hear what he had to say. I could smell his aftershave, which was very different from my sweat, he could smell. I felt embarrassed. I thanked him and headed out across the yard towards our fifth wheel. The school had graciously let us park the RV on the edge of the lot as our finances were dwindling. I opened the fifth wheel door yelling, "I drove on the freeway, I really did and as you can see I was so scared, I perspired until my whole body was soaked."

"Get in the bathroom and take a shower before you catch a cold," Dana said.

I sensed, while being happy for me, she was at the same time worried about her driving. She hadn't been able to learn to drive through all the gears yet. This friend of mine was a school counselor and I had been a teacher before we decided to do this. She was not only a counselor, but she had a master's degree in education. Her of lack coordination and this mental block was very frustrating for her. Also the other members of the class, all men, kept making remarks similar to the words they spoke to me, when I was climbing down off the truck. She takes these remarks to heart. They were particularly mean to her because she had aced our entire written tests. Not to mention their scores were barely passing.

I came out of the bathroom feeling warm and satisfied with myself. My written scores were also higher then all of those in the class, except Dana. I was concerned about her driving, as we planned to experience driving across the country together. We wanted to be the first women driving team. At this time, in 1973 there were a few women driving with their husbands, and prostitutes grabbing a ride for a ride, but no women teams that we knew of driving eighteen-wheelers cross-country.

Dana sat down on the coach and softly muttered, "I must learn to drive. I can't even get to third gear. What in the heck is wrong with me?"

"Stop worrying! You've upset yourself to the point that you can't concentrate on your driving. You have to develop a rhythm when you're double clutching. Stomp with the left foot then shift out of gear, another stomp with the left foot and slip it to the next gear. Ignore looking at the gages and trying to get to the exact revolutions per minute. Shift to the sound of the motor. Try this tomorrow." I said.

Dana said I should stop worrying about her and study for my test and with those harsh words, I knew she didn't want any more advise.

Next day Ted walked to the front of the classroom and shouted, "Listen up and sit down. We have a lot to cover. This week will end classes and next week the Department of Motor Vehicles will be here to give us our road test."

I glanced over at Dana who was looking frustrated.

Ted explained, "This week on Friday all students will drive to Ontario to a truck stop. Once there, students must trade trailers. You will disconnect from your trailer and connect to another student's trailer. Then drive back to the yard.

After class he came to us and asked us to trade trailers with each other. He wanted to stop any problems, which might arise between the typical male drivers and the women drivers. I was worried that we couldn't do this, which I expressed to Dana. When we were out of hearing range of our counterparts, Dana asked me to stop worrying. She said, "Sandy, this isn't going to be a problem. I'm all set to get my rhythm started and we will beat the heck out of them."

"I would love to beat them." I uttered. We giggled together. We went back to the RV. I grabbed the dog leash and called Bugsy for a walk. Bugsy came to us when we were camping at the Lake Havasu. He was very dirty and full of bugs, but very loveable. He was so hungry we bought some dog food for him. When Dana came out of the store, she was carrying a 50-pound bag of dog food.

I took one look and said, "It looks like we have a new traveling companion."

After we ate we went into the yard. We each picked a truck and teacher. I ran into Joe and suggested he might be able to help Dana. Joe was a good teacher who might just be able to do a better job of teaching Dana to drive. He said he would definitely give it his best shot.

I went through the normal check of the truck, climbed up into the cab and started the motor. She hummed like a bird. This school was excellent at keeping up with maintenance of the trucks.

It felt very powerful sitting behind the wheel

of this huge vehicle. It was 60 feet long and 11 feet 4 inches high. I could look in the rearview mirror and see what looked like a train behind me. If I concentrated on how huge the truck was, it scared me. So I would put the size of the truck out of my mind and concentrate on my driving. A driving teacher broke my silence and climbed into the passenger seat. Being short with a rather large stomach, it was hard to imagine him reaching the pedals, or did he wear lifts on his shoes? Oh well, all he had to do is teach me to drive. I didn't have to ride with him driving.

Revving up the motor, I headed for the driveway and out on the road, after stopping at the stop sign, of course. I asked him if we could go to the freeway.

After questioning me about driving up there before, Eddie said, "Let's try it."

Hearing doubt in his voice, encouraged me to do this perfectly. I'm sure I made some mistakes but it was an acceptable ride. He encouraged me to go faster. I thought I was moving fast because the sound of the diesel motor was loud. When I looked at the speedometer it read thirty-seven miles per hour. Wow! These motors are loud. No wonder it damages your ears if you don't cover them up. With some prodding from Eddie, I went about forty-five or fifty. The truck was shaking and rattling, but the seat I was setting on moved along a smooth and straight path. Thank God for air ride seats.

Having finished my lesson we came back into the yard. Dana was in her truck, driving backward and forward, and backward again. I walked back near her.

I shouted , "What's happening?"

Dana responded, "All I know is I've mastered this backing stuff.

I could drive to Albuquerque backwards if need be." Hearing this explanation I went to the fifth-wheel thinking, I wish she could drive forwards as well. I leashed up Bugsy so he and I could walk for a while and went back to the RV where I settled in to do some studying.

Dana soon came stomping in. She couldn't understand why she had to practice backing again. It's very easy once you get the hang of it. We both knew her forward driving was the problem, however she said she drove forward with some success today. She was able to get to sixth over, much higher than ever before.

Next day, Thursday, we were up early and

ready for the written test. It bothered the male students if we finished early, so we agreed to set in our seats until a few of them finished. While we sat there she looked at me with a smile on her face, and It was all I could do not to laugh out loud, but I didn't.

Outside afterwards we decided to go the trucking school office to let them know we would like to apply for jobs. We specified working together and cross-country. By the looks on their faces we surprised them. I guess they assumed we had husbands hidden out somewhere or maybe we were hookers.

They gave us a couple jobs to apply for, but since our lesson to drive too Ontario and swap trailers tomorrow had not happened yet. We agreed we should take the driving test before applying for a job, since the only requirement to drive a truck is a truck driver's license. In the afternoon the teacher brought us back in the classroom. He went over the test and reviewed, and also explained to us all how to drive down a mountain.

"Can you believe this," Dana exclaimed, "The most difficult driving procedure is going down hill and he explains it in class."

I said, "I agree with you, but maybe there is

a hill between here and Ontario. In that case we will use our knowledge on hills tomorrow."

Well I was wrong, so now if we should drive cross-country we will have to try it on our own.

Along came Friday, it was quiet while we ate breakfast and prepared for our first real drive.

I found my truck in the back of the second row next to a student, who always was very irritated because two women were in his driving class. We both started checking out our rigs, as we knew we were supposed to do. He went clock wise and I went counter clock wise, which put us both in the middle of the trucks at the same time. He smiled in a ha-ha way, with only one tooth on top and two on the bottom.

He said, "Girl ya' gona get ya' ass kicked today, cause ya' cain't do this trip. Ya'll can answer questions on a test but that ain't goina help ya' drive. So goodbye to ya'll and good riddance."

I simply gathered up all the guts I could muster to say, "We shall see won't we."

I tried not to look at him any more, as he was making me sick spitting through his teeth. Sometimes spit would catch on the one upper tooth and dangle down.

Unfortunately he was right. We would have to earn a drivers license. He made me more determined to accomplish the goal we came here for.

I was hoping Dana would experience the same thing, thus feeling like I do. She was in the far back of the yard, waiting for everyone else to drive on out of the driveway.

I was pretty nervous sitting in the seat waiting for my teacher to arrive. I decided it would make me feel calmer if I went over some of the details of driving. Pre-occupying my mind really did help. Glen came over and went through the checking of the truck with me. All was well, so we went out of the drive and turned right heading towards the freeway. I was so glad Glen had all his teeth.

We came to the ramp and went up on the freeway. I didn't have quite enough speed to move out into traffic. I squirmed my way out there and fortunately Glen was impressed with how calmly I handled the situation. Driving the rest of the way was pretty simple. We arrived at the truck stop about an hour and a half from the time we left the school. The truck stop looked scary, mainly because there were trucks driving erratically all over the place.

Glen said, "Take it slow and carefully work your way through it. Now go over to the side rode and park. We will wait for Dana there."

Thank goodness Glen was full of old truckers stories, which helped the time pass by. His stories made me anxious to find a driving job, so I could be on the road making my own experiences. I want to finish this class and have my own life as a driver.

Glen finally said, "I'll go into the truck stop to call our school and find out what's happening to Dana."

He came walking back twirling his right arm around, which meant start up the truck. I started the truck and back to the school we headed. When we arrived we could see Dana driving her truck in the back of the yard. She was doing some maneuvers we couldn't figure out. She was backing and angling the trailer at different directions.

I decided to go take Bugsy for his walk. He loved the yard, as there was a section he could run free in. After a while I went in the 5th wheel and started dinner.

A short while later Dana came in and she was in pretty good humor, which surprised me because she hadn't made her trip to Ontario.

She explained, "Joe took me around the block and decided my general driving was good enough to pass the test on Monday. Then he said we all have to drive a blind ninety in the driving test. A ninety is a corner of a building. It is ninety degrees. When you drive a blind ninety; you are backing the trailer around a corner of a building to a parking place at the dock. So he asked me to practice that against the fence in the yard.

It is blind when the trailer swings away from the driver, and with that happening she can't see the trailer in the rearview mirror.

"Is that what you were doing when we came in?" I questioned. I tried not to laugh.

"Yes," She said and laughed herself.

"It sure didn't look like one." I said.

"You came too late," Dana, sputtered, "I drove a couple perfect ones."

"A couple," I shouted, "out of how many?"

Dana said, "Oh maybe thirty-five."

"That's certainly not a good percentage," I said, "but I don't know if I can even do that much."

"Don't worry my friend, it's all been worked out. Joe said the cop who checks our blind ninety's is quite short. So Joe will stand behind the cop and direct us which way to turn the wheel." Dana explained.

"You're kidding!" I said.

"No I'm not. The guys will go out of the yard to take their road test, during which time we will drive our blind nineties." Said Dana.

"Wow, what a break. I sure hope it works." I said.

This idea had calmed Dana down substantially, but not me. I could see many things that could go wrong. I didn't even want to think about it, so I put dinner on plates, so we could eat.

After dinner I went to the trucking books and found a description of doing a blind ninety. Dana finished the dishes and settled to watch television.

After a short while she asked, "What are you doing?"

Answering I said, "I am reading up on doing a blind ninety."

"You don't have to study. The teachers will help us like I explained, so please stop worrying and come relax for a while." She said.

I read until I was finished and watched a little television, then off to bed. It was not hard to sleep, as I was tired and soon sleeping like a babe.

Monday came quickly. Everyone was in the yard. Instead of the usual noise it was quite quiet. Joe was assigning everyone a truck.

After everyone had checked out his or her assigned truck.

Joe announced, "Will all the trucks pull up and stop to let a cop in. except for numbers 2 and 7. When all the rest are on the road test, I'll explain what we want 2 and 7 to do. So, Lets get going!"

It took about fifteen minutes for the male drivers to leave.

The classroom had a porch all around it. On the side by the driveway there was a fence on the opposite side of the drive, which made enough space exactly for a trucker to drive a blind ninety and end up with the back of the trailer up against the fence and the front facing the porch, with about three feet to spare.

Joe called for number seven, (Dana) to turn her truck around and back towards the space between the deck and the fence. Then, of course, She was asked to do a blind ninety.

Joe was in his spot casually standing behind Richard, the cop. She looked at Joe, who was waving her backwards into the spot closer to the porch than the fence. He swung his right arm clockwise over Richard's head. Dana copied the move with her steering wheel, which was a counter clockwise movement for Dana. The trailer swung around to the right. Joe stopped swinging his arm, but Dana didn't stop turning for a couple moments. This made the cab and trailer jackknife. He then directed her forward, which pulled her out of the jackknife, but was not at all near a ninety turn. Now he swung his arm counter clockwise, she followed and again did this way to long. The truck was now about forty-five degrees from the fence. He directed her forward again a time or two, and she always ended at an angle far less than ninety degrees.

Richard said, "Let her go out on the road and bring in number two."

I had already turned my truck around. I was so glad she was first because it help me to see her mistakes. I thought I should watch him all the time so I would know when to stop a certain direction. We went through the ritual twice. I had created an angle of about eighty degrees. My real mistake was not stopping soon enough, and backing into the fence, which knocked it partially over. It had to be fixed so the guys could do their ninety's. I was sure we had both failed.

The driving around two blocks of the school, wouldn't be hard because we all drove on these roads during class. When my turn was finished I drove into the yard through the second driveway, away from all the action.

I saw Dana on the porch and went up to meet her. She was holding some papers in her hand. Her smile told me all was well, just as she shouted, "We made it!"

"Me too?" I questioned.

"Yes, both of us, we passed." Dana shouted.

Then we heard several negative comments from a group of the other students.

We were so happy we ignored them like we had done during the whole class. We were both so happy and smiling that these pictures were the best DMV pictures we've ever taken.

Walking out Dana spoke, "The first big hurdle was over and the second about to start."

Chapter 2

I gradually woke up and opened my eyes. Then remembering I'm a professional driver brought a smile to my face. One would not think coming from a professional teaching position, a license to drive an eighteen-wheeler would mean so much. However, driving across our country and earning a living at the same time, is something I have always dreamed of doing.

Dana was making some waking noises in the other room. I got up and prepared to get some breakfast around. Our discussion at breakfast, took on the question of how to get a job.

I asked if we should dress up?

Dana answered, "Are you kidding? We could never get a trucking job wearing a dress. If we dressed like a ho we could, but that isn't the kind of job we want."

I said, "We should probably go into the office and ask their opinion."

Remember that part of this contract is for the school to find a job for us. Since they didn't teach us how to drive down a mountain, the

least they could do is find us a job so we can kill ourselves in the mountains." We laugh at that and decided to head to the office.
Surprise! We came out of there with a possible job offer.

We drove off to a truck stop in LA. The office even had them both meet us in the lobby of the same truck stop.

We walked into the lounge in our slacks and blouses. Two men walked over to us and asked if we were Dana and Sandy.

"We sure are." we echoed together.

Then Dana turned to me and asked if I would talk to one and she would talk to the other to save time. That's what we did. My guy was not as bad as the fellow with one tooth on the top jaw, but he could have showered and shaved. Any way he said, "Let's go out to my truck."

I followed him, while an uneasy feeling was beginning to develop in my mind. I asked if he always did his interviews in his truck. His answered scared me.

He said, "Only if its a women."

I said, "Are you really looking for a driver or something else."

He answered, "Why not both?"

I said, "I've heard enough." in a very loud voice. I headed for the lounge again, and half way up the steps I ran into Dana. I could tell by her body language she was also very angry.

She asked, "Did he want a job or a ho?"

"Both" I said, "However, he said I wouldn't have to drive much."

Needless to say, we headed straight back to the trucking school. I let Dana handle it cause she could put on a much bigger and louder case then I could. She stormed around in there for about fifteen minutes, then coming out of the office,

She yelled in a very high voice, "Don't you ever send us for an interview like that again."

She slammed the door behind her. She grabbed my arm and pulled me with her.

Back in the fifth wheel we each took refuge in our own separate corner of this very small living quarters. The space between us felt appropriate because our feelings made us feel like being completely alone.

Bugsy took a spot in the middle of the floor and sort of hovered down with his head on the linoleum.

I drifted of to sleep and later woke up hungry. Dana wasn't there, I knew she would be walking Bugsy.

When she came back she was much calmer, so I asked her if she wanted to go out for dinner. We both thought it was a good idea.

Smelling and sipping a glass of wine before dinner relaxed us to the point we could start discussing what we should do now. She told me the women in the office pointed out, if we were adamant about driving together, we would have to go to big companies, who had several rigs and hired people to drive them. I felt this would be a good idea, but very hard to do. Of all the companies around the Los Angeles area, none of them had an all women team. Going home it was quiet in the pick-up truck. My mind was on the difficult task ahead and just how we should approach it.

Next morning, during breakfast, there was a knock on the door. I answered it and saw Cornelia, a women who worked in the office. We asked her to come in and have a seat.

She immediately started with apologies, "We didn't have much of a choice of jobs for you. None of the big companies have a women team and the two we talked to said, "No, not just no, but absolutely not!"

"This morning we found three who agreed to interview you. Here are their address's and phone numbers. They are aware of the fact that you will call them. We didn't mean to imply that you were prostitutes. We just didn't have any companies listed that wanted to talk to an all women team." She left on a good note, but she had just let us know the difficulty of our next hurdle.

We set up our interviews. Since two interviews were rather close together, we decide to go to those two today and the other one tomorrow.

The first company said no with a smirk. The second just said no and wished us luck.

The next day we went to the third, a cross-country shipping company. Mr. Baker explained they didn't need any drivers, however, they had an individual who leases five trucks to them and he might need a team. He called Fred Stenger to say we were here and would he like to come over to talk to us?

We made ourselves comfortable on a picnic table in a small grassy area.

I ran my hand across the top of the table and picked up a splinter in my hand. It was bleeding profusely when Fred arrived and set down with us. It wasn't much of an interview, but it was the best one we've had. He checked to see if we had confidence in our driving. Also, he asked questions about driving a truck. One question was do we know how to drive down a mountain?

I said, "Yes", then I proceeded to quote from the driving class book of how to drive down a mountain. After a few more questions he stated that he didn't have an opening now, but maybe in the near future he might. As he walked away I watched until he was gone and then let out a big,

"OOOWWHHUUU, AND AN OUCH VERY LOUD!"

Then I lifted my hand to show huge puddle of blood.

Dana said, "Oh my gosh, why didn't you get up and go to the bathroom."

"Do you think he would hire a wimpy woman to drive his truck?" I said.

"No, you did the right thing." She said.

I immediately went into a bathroom to clean my hand.

I said, "I'm certainly glad my hand didn't drip visible blood while we were talking to him.

We left from there with the most hope for getting a job in a long time.

On the way home, Dana said, "You gave Fred the idea that we have driven down a mountain."

"No I didn't! He didn't ask if we have driven down a mountain, he asked if we know how to drive down a mountain. We both know how because we've read it."

Dana, "That's sort of splitting hairs, don't you think?"

"Maybe, but I feel confident we could handle it." I defended myself.

We kept looking for a job, we read the want adds in the LA paper. We also went to truck stops to read the bulletin boards and talk to the drivers. We met some drivers who were a lot cleaner and nicer than our school friends. Some were even encouraging. So we kept looking for a job by reading ads, discussing jobs with drivers, and letting it be known that we would do anything, except prostitution.

After two weeks, we realized we had covered about everything that could be found in the LA area.

When we first came to California, we found an RV Park in the San Diego area, which we both loved, so this made it easy to determine where to go next.

We hooked up the fifth wheel and said good-by to everyone. I saw Joe sitting on the porch and drifted over there to thank him very much for helping us.

He smiled, "I'll keep an ear open for a job for you. I hope you keep on trying, cause persistence works. Good by and good luck."

Heading for Lemon Grove, a small town near San Diego was a great feeling. We were finally getting out of that trucking school-yard. Also, I had a trucking license in my purse.

Setting up the fifth wheel went fast. The man next door observed that Bugsy was bigger than before. I didn't notice his growth because it happened so slowly. I only hope he will be comfortable in a truck.

Dana and I started our search for a driving job again, much like we had in LA. Only this time, we took some relief from it, to have some fun and explore San Diego. Riding our bikes in Balboa Park, visiting some artsy places, hitting golf balls, going to movies, and eating fish down on the wharf, are a few of the experiences we enjoyed.

   Before we realized it, October had come and gone, then November, and soon it was December. Many nights I lay there in bed, listening to the trucks climbing the huge mountain foothill behind our RV Park. I would guess what gear the driver was in and wish I was driving the truck, so I could double clutch into the next gear.

Dana and I were trying to decide how to spend Christmas. Our Thanksgiving celebration would not be appropriate for Christmas. We had gone to our favorite Mexican Restaurant. We sat in the bar portion and ordered a pitcher of marguerites. The bartender had become friends with us over time and new we were on a tight budget. He would ask the waitress to bring us some chips and salsa.

These marguerites were the best I've ever had. So this was our Thanksgiving dinner.

Christmas must be a little more special than our unusual Thanksgiving. Since we were in San Diego, the wharf would be appropriate. This made our decision very easy because our favorite restaurant was on the wharf. We would order shrimp cocktail and beer and set on the back deck of the restaurant, which faced the ocean. You could watch the sun go down from there. It was peaceful and beautiful on the deck.

It was December the twenty-third, we were sitting out side the fifth wheel in a small area set up for Bugsy, when the phone rang. Dana was closest to the door and jumped up running into the fifth wheel to answer the phone.

I heard her yell, "YES! YES! We will be there."

I went in and she was writing down an address. She hung up the phone and yelled, "WE HAVE A JOB! WE HAVE A JOB!"

We both jumped up and down and

gave high fives.

I asked, "Who is it with?"

"Do you remember the guy who interviewed us at the picnic table, when you scraped a splinter off the top of the table into your hand?" she said.

"Yes, and it's with him right?" I asked. "Yes," she answered, "I don't know anything except we have to be at his house tomorrow morning at 9 o'clock."

"But tomorrow is Christmas Eve," I said.

"I know and that is the only reason we have the job. His driver will be arriving into Los Angeles tomorrow and doesn't want to go back out again. Fred has another load to go out, so we can have it if we will take it tomorrow," She said.

I shouted, "WE WILL! WE WILL! So much for Christmas on the wharf, but this will be better."

Chapter 3

Waking up at 5:00 am was not our cup of tea. We had been off work for seven months and getting up this early was no longer in our schedule. It was so exciting to have a driving job, we soon forgot how early it was and headed our pick-up towards Los Angeles.

Arriving fifteen minutes early, Mrs. Stenger answered the door. She was a little surprised to see two women standing there. Obviously, she expected two men.

Fred came down the stairs of his duplex, said his hellos, and told his wife to make pancakes. The first pancake he demanded, so we waited for ours.

At the table, Fred began explaining the situation to us. CJ, the driver, has two small kids and wanted to spend Christmas with them. I couldn't allow this because of my finances. He didn't say how bad his finances were, just that they were tight. Knowing this, I had mixed feelings about taking the job. I took some time to think about it. When it hit me, CJ could easily find another place to work and we couldn't, so I knew we should accept the job.

Now the fun begins. CJ was supposed to arrive in the afternoon on Christmas Eve. The afternoon went by without a phone call from him. Fred was becoming angrier about every hour that slipped by. About 11:00 pm the phone rang. After the call, Fred came into the living room and let us know, CJ was in town and hid the rig, so no one else could drive it back out. The call was from CJ's buddy, who also drove for Fred, and wanted to keep his job.

Fred said in a harsh voice, "Get your belongings, Bugsy, and park your truck in the side drive. We are going to Ontario to find my truck and trailer."

Fred's wife, pulled us aside, to say she was very glad Fred was giving us a chance to drive. She then wished us luck. She didn't realize how much luck we would need.

Fred, and a friend he picked up, the two of us, and Bugsy, headed for Ontario. This friend was an amateur electrician. Fred had sensed that CJ might damage the truck somehow.

It was a long way to Ontario. Dana and I were very tired. We had been up since five o'clock. It was now near 1:00 AM Christmas Day. As Fred kept driving around Ontario from one business to another, looking for his rig, I fell asleep.

Suddenly he slammed on his brakes, waking me up, and checked out his trailer, which was tightly backed up against a building.

Fred came back and said, "Well, he did a good job of placing the trailer so no one could steal the goods from it, but where in hell is my tractor?"

I went back to sleep. I didn't know how long I had been asleep and when I woke up. I saw a tractor beside the gravel road we were on.

Fred tried to start the truck, and found his suspicions were correct. He called Jim, the electrician, to help him because the CB radio had been yanked out. All the wires, connected to the radio were strip, and left hanging out of the CB compartment. Fred and Jim worked together for about forty-five minutes, jumped down and gave the keys to us.

We put our clothes and Bugsy in the cab, when we heard Fred say, "Who will drive?"

I quickly answered, "I will."

I climbed up into the drivers seat noticing this was not at all like the trucks we had been trained on. Fortunately, it was designed close enough that I could start it up and shift.

Fred had given us the papers for his load, which had to be picked up in Los Angeles. He followed us for a short way and then took off.

What a relief, no one was following us and we were on our first job. Dana pulled out the map to find the way to our load.

In about an hour we drove into the yard to pick up the loaded trailer.

Dana climbed out and went into the little cage building where the guard was sleeping. She woke him to ask which load was ours. He pulled out the bill of laden and handed it to her. I was anxious to see where we were going, so I went in also.

Dana questioned the guard, "This goes to Philadelphia?"

I questioned him also, "The one in Pennsylvania?"

He said, "Yes, is there another one?" he then asked, "How long have you two been driving?"

To which I answered, "Two years, where is the trailer?"

He pointed to it and set down again.

I drove the truck over to the trailer and Dana walked. I couldn't believe how the trailer was parked. It was on a ramp, which was about 40 degrees down, and up against the dock.

Dana looked up at me and said, "I've never seen a dock like this, have you?"

"No! It surely will make the connection difficult." I said.

I turned the truck around and backed up to where the ramp started, I stopped and climbed out of the cab. We were walking around the truck to determine the best way to connect to this trailer. Dana started cranking the trailer up higher, so the truck would slip under it. She walked out of the ramp and waved me back.

I knew the trick of this would be to go very slow, so I could take my foot off the gas and on the brake quickly. I started back, then I heard Dana scream, "STOP! STOP!"

I quickly put my foot on the brake, just before the fifth wheel crashed into the trailer. I put it in first gear and went forward up out of the ramp.

Dana came over to say, "The pin on the trailer is a little to the left of where you had the fifth wheel. I will crank the trailer up a little higher. Next time go slower and I will walk along the side of the truck to direct you."

I started back slower and found that if I put the gear stick in reverse, I could keep my foot on the brake, letting the cab roll backwards and stop it quickly if need be. I followed Dana's directions and heard the fifth wheel and pin of the trailer connect with a loud bang. The guard was watching us from his shack, like a vulture flying over road kill. Both Dana and I knew he was looking for a mistake. This made us even more adamant to connect the tractor and trailer quickly and correctly, just to show him we could.

Dana was connecting the air hoses and checking the lock on the fifth wheel.

I said to her, as I dropped out of the cab, "Let's not crank the jacks all the way up, because if the trailer drops off of the fifth wheel, for some reason, it won't fall all the way down."

She said, "Good idea and let's both check everything, to prevent a mistake."

I replied, "We make a good team."

We both yelled, "Yes," then gave high fives.

I checked everything also, then climbed in put the gear stick in first gear and gave her gas. It didn't move an inch. I tried it again and didn't go anywhere. I had never pulled a trailer with a load in it, so I wasn't sure how it should feel. I tried it again with a lot of gas. It didn't go anywhere. By this time I could smell hot motor. Then I remembered Joe had explained the gears to me and said there is a granny gear to use for extra torque. I put the truck in granny gear and up the ramp we went.

Before Dana cranked the jacks all the way up I put on the trailer brakes and tried to pull the cab forward. This is the third check of the lock on the fifth wheel. We were securely fastened.

Dana climbed in and said, "let's get out of here."

As I drove by the guard shack, I blew the air horn and waved. The guard was dozing off and jumped nearly out of his chair. We both giggled like teen-age boys. After all, this was our new truck. We both seemed very happy.

Dana directed us back to the ten Freeway. Once there, we headed east. I found it very different to drive with a full load. The amount of time I had to shift and double shift was very much shorter, as the load pulled the trailer back in between shifts.

Obviously the load would pull backwards, making it difficult to get the revolutions per minute up to the correct place to make a shift.

I was wondering how Dana would adapt to the difference. I didn't make any comments about it, so she wouldn't be worrying about it until she drove.

Dana spoke, "Do you remember reading the part in the truck driving book, which said we should weigh the load before going to far, as it should be within the law of load weights?"

"Yes, I read that. Should we stop in the truck stop in Ontario? I noticed a small scale there. It looked like one, which could only weigh one axle at a time."

"Yes, Lets stop there." Dana answered.

I was getting so tired. I could hardly hold my head up, let alone drive. We finally came to the truck stop. It was empty, unlike the first time I was here. I drove over to the scales and leaned out the window to make sure I had the front axle completely on the scale. It was about two hundred pounds overweight. I drove forward so the next set of axles would be on the scales. This automatically drove the front axle off the scale. The second axles were also higher than they should be. We were elated to find the third set of axles 33,000 pounds instead of 34,000 pounds.

The job ahead was one we read about, but hadn't practiced. The last two sets of axles where on sliding rails. There was a lock on each one, which had to be unlocked, so the axle could slide to a different position.

    First we tried to lower the weight on the front axle by unlocking the second axle. Then put the brakes on the back axle and drove backward. This would slide the second axle forward. Dana locked it up again. I drove over to the scales again and the first was fine.

    Since we where all set up, we weighed all three axles. The second was very much over weight. The third was about the same as before.

    To lower the weight on the second axle we had to unlock the third one, put the brakes on, then back up sliding the last axle closer to the front of the trailer. This would cause it to take part of the weight off the second axle.

    Again we weighed all three axles and found that all three were over the allotted amount for the highway regulations. We then slid the second axle back where it had been and put the last axle back also. Now at least we had only two axles that were over weight. That would be the second axle and the first.

We both were so tired, we couldn't think any more.

Dana said, "For our health's sake we should rent one of these truck stop rooms and get some sleep."

"Good Idea," I said. "We made it all the way to Ontario from Los Angeles on our first driving day." Being extremely tired, we both burst out laughing. This all seemed so out of character for us.

I put the truck in line with the other trucks. Walking to the truck stop, with our bedding and pillows under our arms, we started to get into an uncontrollable laugh. I had to go to the bathroom, but we couldn't stop laughing. It had to be four in the morning or so and we were walking across the empty parking lot in an Ontario truck stop. I started running and Dana followed. I headed into the truck stop, through the restaurant and straight to the women's bathroom. Dana followed.

She said, "I'm sure glad this is a two holler."

It took a while to gain control, get up and walk to the room. The room was four cement walls, no windows, only a door.

The bathroom was down the hall. There were two narrow beds, which we threw our sleeping bags and pillows on. We had left Bugsy in the truck. He had the best bed of all.

After we settled down I asked, "Which Christmas do you think is the best. This one or shrimp cocktail and beer on the dock?" The uncontrollable laughter took over us again. My stomach ached and soon I fell asleep.

We woke up about ten o'clock am. We took turns showering. It was Christmas Day, so there weren't many truckers here. This made it easy to shower in this trucker's motel without getting interrupted, then we ate breakfast.

While eating we discussed which route to take.

Dana said, "I have a friend in Phoenix and would like to see her."

I answered, "Yes that sounds good. It will be slower, and I don't think there are as many mountainous roads going to Flagstaff on the route from Phoenix."

"What do you think we should do about the weight problem of the trailer?" I asked.

We agreed that one of us should call Fred, but who should it be? I agreed to call him. He answered the phone kind of gruffly. I told him that his load is over weight and asked what should be done about it.

He said, "Nothing, just drive it to the destination. Then he added this is a holiday week and there won't be any weigh stations open. So just drive."

"I agree to drive, if you will pay any tickets or fines for being over weight." I said.

I have no idea where my unexpected guts came from.

After a few swear words he agreed and we prepared to drive, after we bought two log books. The law says we have to keep a log of when we drive and when we sleep.

Walking out to the truck I asked Dana if she would drive.

"No not yet," she mumbled.

After checking out the truck, I climbed in the drivers seat and we went out across the desert towards Phoenix. It was very cold and a strong wind was blowing. I was glad we had a warm comfortable cab to reside in.

Looking at the dash, I new I didn't understand all the dials and buttons.

I asked Dana, "Will you see if there is a book on this truck somewhere, because I would like to know what these dials and buttons are for."

Dana found a manual of the truck in the side pocket. She carefully went through all the dials and buttons and their functions. I was relieved to see her memorizing them as well as I, because it seems as though she really does plan to drive.

It took most of the way to Wilameana's apartment, to learn this different truck's functions.

On the way there, we stopped to eat in a truck stop. Spotting a small comfortable room with "Drivers" written over the door, we walked in kind of timidly and sat at the counter. A waitress came over to tell us we couldn't eat here because this is for the drivers. This seemed pretty strange, as there were only two other drivers in the place.

Dana spoke up, "We are drivers."

The waitress said, "Where are your log books?"

I said, "In the truck!"

The waitress said, "You're kidding. I'll need to see them if you want to eat."

Dana said, "I'll get them." She walked out and brought them back with her.

The waitress angrily tossed the menus to us. At this point I was mystified as to why she was so angry. I guess it was because she didn't want to be wrong or didn't want any competition for the male drivers.

As time went on in our travels, we found the people we met would either like the fact we were women drivers, or disliked it immensely. There didn't seem to be any middle ground. I had just found out first hand what it must have felt like to be a black person in the South earlier. Not totally, because they couldn't run out to the truck to get a logbook.

We drove on to Wilameana's home. Who would name their kid Wilameane? These are just my thoughts, which I surely wouldn't say out loud.

Thank goodness there was an empty lot out behind Wila's apartment. I pulled into it with ease, just like old times in the truck yard. I sat back and relaxed for a while. Dana jumped out to go see her friend.

After a short while they walked back to the truck. I could hear Wila scolding her friend fiercely.

I heard Wila's voice, "You have a master's degree. You had an excellent job and now your driving this truck. What's wrong with your head?"

At the sound of Wila's anger I jumped out of the truck and introduced myself to her and a couple other people standing there. There was a little fuss over Bugsy. Then I tied him under the trailer and we walked towards the apartment.

Wila said, "I have some left over's from Christmas dinner. Would you like to eat with us?"

"I would like that very much." I said.

After dinner I excused myself to go sleep in the cab, with Bugsy. Dana asked if I would sleep in the apartment. She didn't want to be harassed again. I told her I should get some quality sleep and also we should get started early. So I answered, "I will sleep in the truck."

I added, "Trucks aren't supposed to stop at night, they just change drivers Hint, Hint.

Chapter 4

I started driving about nine o'clock the next morning. We were headed towards Flagstaff, which I found was very much up hill. Of course, what had I been thinking, if Flagstaff is approximately 7,280 feet above sea level and Phoenix is desert, we had to go up hill. First foot hills and then mountains.

Driving along seemed easier than I thought it would be. I guess the reason for that is, the roads are new, wide, and quite straight. Compared to the other route, from Kingman, to Flagstaff, which I didn't feel ready for yet.

The little hills were very good practice hills; and then we came to a sign, which read;

"ALL TRUCKS STOP AT PULL OVER TO CHECK BRAKES"

We both echoed, "Oh my God"

I quickly pulled the truck over, put on the brakes and we set there quietly, with a look of what have we done, on our faces. Why did we get ourselves into this?

I climbed out of the truck and started walking around it with the tire bumper in my hand. I bumped all tires, even the spare.

Dana checked the air hose connections to make sure they were tight. Everything looked fine, so we climbed back in.

I said to Dana, "I'm going to recap to you the directions of how to drive down a mountain. Please let me know if it is the same rendition you read, with nothing left out."

I spoke, "I must stay in a low gear, like second gear. When the speed goes up to a point where the revolutions per minute are around 2100, I push hard on the brakes so the speed goes way down quickly, and the revolutions per minute with it. I can then take my foot off the brake completely and let the truck go back up to the same spot on the revolutions per minute dial, then repeat this action. This keeps my foot off the brake continuously, which would cause the brakes to over heat.

At some point the speed will jump from the slow end to the 2100 revolutions per minute end quite quickly. Then I must shift to the next higher gear. This will extend the time again. If I do this repetition to the highest gear and the revolutions per minutes are at 2100 again, and I have no higher gear to go to, I will have two choices. One is to take the truck ramp, created to stop the truck because it is totally filled with sand. Two, is to pull the truck up against a mountain wall or cliff until it stops. Scraping the whole right side of the trailer and truck."

Dana speaks, "You didn't have to go that far. If you are trying to scare me, you have accomplished your goal."

I answered, "Good cause you can't possibly be as scared as I am. I have to drive this huge damn thing down that mountain. There is one little thing I left out. Before the speed gets very high and I can still bring it down to a slow pace. I can then pull it over on the side of the road, stop and let the brakes cool. Then start out slow again.

Dana said, "Thanks for that little tidbit."

"OK, Here we go," I said, I pulled out of the brake check area very slowly and preceded to execute the procedure I had just described. All went fine for quite a while. The slant of this hill wasn't as steep as I expected.

Another thing that made it easier was I could see the road up hill across the valley. It was straight as an arrow.

I eventually realized trucks were flying by us one after another. Obviously I should relax and let it go all out that is put it in neutral. This extra speed would even help us get up the next hill.

To which Dana screamed, "What are you doing? Slow down NOW!"

I explained to her what I was doing and she settled down a little.

At the top of the next hill I stopped and both of us got out. I walked over to her and said, "Give me a high five", which she did.

We both sat down on a log to cool off again. I was just as wet with sweat, as I had been the first time I drove on the freeway.

We both were getting over a little of our fear and beginning to feel a sense of accomplishment. I walked around the brake check area. At one point I could see through the bushes, what looked like a seven on a half hidden sign. My heart sunk. I walked back toward Dana, as I didn't want her to see this percentage of slope just yet. I might not be able to get her back into the truck. I surely did not want to do this alone.

I sat down beside her again and thought it is time to get started.

I said, "I don't know what the correct amount of time is for carrying a load cross country, but I am sure we are way behind. So let's get going. I know after Flagstaff there isn't any long down hill sprints, so it should get easier from there for a while."

She said, "O K", reluctantly.

We both got into the truck, as I said a quiet prayer for us. Sometimes there is an advantage to the loud noise of the motor. I pulled us out on the roadway. There was a curve first thing.

Dana shouted, "This is a seven percent slope!"

"It's all right we will make it just like we did the last one," I answered.

Thank God this first curve was at the beginning of the hill, cause our speed was still very slow. It was easy to manipulate the curve. Then I saw the next curve was longer and sharper, so I put on the brakes and slowed us way down. My heart began beating very fast and my hands where gripping the steering wheel super tight. We made it quite nicely around the second curve. Thank God I slowed the truck down in between those two straight road ways. Next there was a down hill to what looked like a bridge at the bottom. Then the road went straight back up another hill.

Dana was yelling again, "Look at that little bridge down there. I don't think we will fit on it."

"Sure we will it only looks little because it's so far away," I answered.

Dana asked, "What if another car or truck comes?"

I had to concentrate on getting the truck down safely.

I said, "Please calm yourself down, so I can do this job. Your not even thinking clearly, because if you were you would know that this is a freeway, so no other vehicles will be on our side coming toward us."

At that point, I was about to put on the brakes to bring the speed and the revolutions per minute down. I was beginning to see, when you can keep the speed down this way,

I almost didn't have to shift up, maybe only a time or two. Realizing this fact really made me confident. I now could handle all hills this way and never needed to worry again. At least all straight hills I could run without worry. We reached about half way down the hill, and knowing the up slope of the mountain road was completely straight, I slipped her into neutral as I could hear Dana say, "Oh no here we go again."

I looked over at Dana and she was white as a sheet.

I said, "You need to calm your self down and think more clearly or you will have a heart attack. When you feel yourself getting panicky and unreasonable and scared, catch those feelings and stop them. Now, see how big the bridge is, you could fit a 747 airplane and us on it. Actually this is kind of fun."

She shouted, "If you tell anyone what I said about the bridge, I swear I'll hurt you badly."

"I promise I won't, but you should start recognizing when you are slipping into a panic and stop it. If you need to talk to me about it that is just fine. However try to talk to me before I get into a ninety-two mile an hour run down a mountain grade." I begged her.

We reached the peak of that grade just fine and reaching across the doghouse we gave ourselves another high five.

Bugsy all this time was tormented. He didn't know whether to go hide in the back behind the flap, which folds down between the front of the cab and the bed, or come out to stand on the doghouse.

I found it interesting the real name for the big protrusion between the driver's seat and the passenger is "doghouse". It really is a piece of metal, which covers the motor, because this truck is a COE, which means cab over engine. So when Bugsy came to the front of the truck, he stood on the doghouse. I'm never sure if his terrible shaking is from the truck's shaking or because he was scared. It is probably a little of both.

During our mountain climbing episodes he would mainly come to the front when our voices rose to a very loud level.

The rest of the way to Flagstaff was uneventful compared to beginning. It was dark when we arrived. There was a nice truck stop to the right so we headed there.

We filled the truck up with diesel and went to the restaurant.

On our way I asked Dana if she knew the appropriated time a trucker should take to reach his destination on the other side of the United States?

Dana said, "I don't know, so maybe we should ask one of truckers in the restaurant."

This was a very nice restaurant. Even the truckers looked a lot cleaner and well dressed. Either we were getting used to them or many of them were not so bad. Any way we picked one out sitting closed to us and inquired about the correct time it should take to get from Los Angeles to Philadelphia.

He chuckled and said, "Three days would be very acceptable. How are you doing?"

Dana quickly said, "We are doing just fine. We should be on time with a little to spare. We grinned at each other and went on eating. On our way back to the truck I told Dana I couldn't drive any longer and we must keep the truck moving.

She said, "Ah and she stalled. There is something you should know. I only have had two wrecks in my life and both of them were after dark. I tend to fall asleep."

I yelled, "WELL NOW ISN'T THIS A GREAT TIME TO TELL ME! Are you planning to drive at all?"

Dana said timidly, "Yes, but I shouldn't start out in the dark and especially as tired as I am right now. It wouldn't be safe. I don't want to lose our lives."

With that explanation I calmed down a bit, but knew we would have to do some planning from now on so Dana wouldn't have to drive late at night when she was tired. With some more thought I suggested we try to get some sleep in the back of the cab. This wouldn't be easy because the bed was a single. How in the world would two people and one big dog fit on a single bed. It wasn't easy.

Dana laid on her right side. I laid on my left and the dog was on our legs. It was very cold outside, close to zero degrees, so I had to keep the motor running. This would supposedly keep the heater on. There was a lot of twisting and turning, so no one was getting much sleep, but we kept trying.

Soon the dog went out on the doghouse for a while. That made this attempt to sleep a little easier. It started to get cold in the cab.

The motor had to be kept running at a higher revolution per minute, in order to keep the heater warm, otherwise it blew cold air. I climbed up front and put my foot on the gas. It was warming up again, however I couldn't stay there. I tried to think of a way to keep pressure on the gas pedal without putting my foot on it. I climbed out of the cab and looked in the small storage space for something heavy. There was a toolbox, which looked like a tackle box. I carried it up in the front seat of the cab. I placed it the long way on the gas pedal. This seemed to work, so I was about to get back in bed, when I realized Bugsy was in my spot. I pushed her out and she fought me all the way. I was lying on my left side with my arms hanging over the side of the bed.

I was so tired I fell asleep in that position. I don't know how long I slept, and was awakened by being very cold almost freezing again. The jiggling of the truck motor caused the toolbox to slowly slide down the gas pedal, so the heater was cold again.

I new I had to have some sleep, so I woke Dana to explain what was happening and asked her to switch places, so she could manipulate the toolbox.

She moaned and I heard her whisper, "Are we having fun yet?" Then she moved up in the front part of the bed to manipulate the toolbox. I don't know how she arranged it, but somehow it stayed in position long enough so we could get some sleep.

This position was so much more comfortable than being in front I actually fell sound asleep.

Chapter 5

We both jumped up, hearing Bugsy bark very loudly at two truckers, who were walking past the front windows, going towards the restaurant. It was a very rude awakening, literal. I looked around to see it was just about dawn.

Dana said, "Why don't we grab a bite and get started driving for the day?"

"Good idea. I don't think we will go to sleep like this again anyway." I answered.

We sat up feeling quite miserable after last night. Dana climbed out and tied Bugsy out on a chain under the trailer. We took some clean clothes and our bags into the restaurant ladies room. Of course there wasn't a shower, but even putting water on our faces felt so good, we proceeded to take as much of a bath in the sink as we could. Putting on clean clothes made us feel almost human again.

We had a fast breakfast and walked towards the truck. I asked Dana if she would like to drive.

She said, "I am embarrassed to say this but, please give me one good rest before I start driving."

Reluctantly I said, "I will this time, but you must start driving soon. Let me tell you it gets easier as you do it. I've learned more out here in these few days than the two weeks in class.

Even though outside it was extremely cold, I found the view extremely beautiful. There were ponderosa pines all along the highway, with some snow on the green limbs. The contrast was striking. I was happy to be driving again. This is what I had dreamed of. Driving through this scenery of mountains and beautiful contrast of colors. The hills were not steep, but gently rolling downward, then a little up grade, and another downward slope. These undulating hills were an easy transition from the 7000 feet above sea level to the prairie below. I noticed the farther I went the smaller the trees were getting. The vegetation was more like high desert.

I drove on for quite some time, admiring the changing scenes. Now my view was prairie, which was level without much vegetation. Off in the distance from the highway, were very striking cliffs. If you used your imagination they looked liked books on a shelf. I probably saw this image because I had been a schoolteacher. It all seemed so long ago.

I reached for the gearstick in an attempt to shift. Something was wrong. It felt very lose. It wouldn't go into another gear.

I hollered, "Dana wakeup, the gearstick is broken."

Dana mumbled, "That's ridicules, gearstick's don't brake. This is a truck!"

I yelled back at her, "It's broken, it's laying on the doghouse.

She answered, "You worry to much. Gearstick's don't break on a truck."

I picked up the gearstick and threw it in the back on top of her. She shouted, "OH MY GOD! THE GEARSTICK BROKE OFF! WHAT ARE WE GOING TO DO?" She came up in the front carrying the gearstick.

"HOW ARE YOU SHIFTING?" She shouted.

I answered, "I'm not, because, you have the gearstick in your hand."

"What are we going to do now?" She said.

"The only thing we can do is drive in this gear until it comes to a point where I have to shift and just let it coast until it stops." I said.

I looked up and saw a sign that read, "WELCOME TO NEW MEXICO."

I said, "Dana we are coming into New Mexico. There is a sign way up ahead about a weigh station, but I can't read it from here." Then because of a slight up grade I knew I should shift, but couldn't. Our speed was beginning to slow down and I could do nothing about it. I could now see the weigh station sign, which read, "New Mexico Entry Weigh and Check Station."

Dana spoke, "Oh, Wouldn't you know, we are coming to a stop right out in front of the New Mexico Entry Port weigh station. Thank God the port looks empty and closed."

The truck stopped and all we could do for a moment was sit there wondering what to do next.

Dana finally said, "This is not all bad, because maybe there is a pay phone in the back of the weigh station for truckers to use. Let's get our boots out of the side storage because we don't know how deep the snow is here."

While we put our boots on, Bugsy was jumping around in the snow, running through it, and enjoying himself tremendously. The three of us started walking across the snow. I could feel the freezing wind hit my face. I put my gloved hands up to cover it. We were about half the way to the station and saw a truck coming towards our truck out on the road and it was slowing down.

All three of us run back towards our truck as fast as we could in these boots. The driver parked his truck behind ours. He jumped down from his seat and we met up with him half way.

He asked, "What's the problem?"

We both started talking, so I stopped and let her handle it. She told him that our gearstick broke off. He started laughing, which brought us all to a laugh. He then took charge, telling us we had to raise the cab. We looked kind of hopeless, cause we had never done this.

He said, "Since the cab will tip way up in the air on it's nose, you have to remove everything from it that will fall out."

We were both so happy to have help, we climbed up and tossed the lose things out. He started to disconnect the cab, which we watched carefully. He went to the front of the truck and jumped up on the bumper. Then he leaned way back using his weight to flip the cab up. It tipped up quite high and things began to fall out. We didn't care about that because we were being help out here. It was still very cold with a strong wind. The wind would at times catch the cab and shake it to the point I thought it might fall off. I heard something fall with a small clink on the road.

The truck driver said, "Boy are you lucky. The pin that clips onto the gearstick and holds it in place, just fell out on the road."

Dana and I both smiled and the trucker began to put the gearstick and pin back together. It only took about a half hour, and then we put the cab back down and fastened it in position. We both expressed how thankful we were and tried to pay him. He refused and then asked us to pay it forward. This was the first time I had heard this expression. He told us the only payment he would accept would be for us to stop the next time we saw a truck stopped on the side of the road, and see if we could help him. This made me feel a lot safer and not so alone out here.

    I asked, "What is your name?"

    "Bill" He said, "and you two?"

    Dana said, "I'm Dana and she is Sandy."

    Bill asked, "Do you have handles?"

    We both looked dumb founded to which he said. "You know, your name you use on your CB radio."

    I said, "We don't have a CB because the driver who had this truck before us ripped it out and took it with him."

    Bill said, "You should really get a CB, as it's impossible to drive safely without one. It can help you with many things that happen out here and make life on the road much easier."

"What's your handle?" Dana asked.

"I'm Wild Bill on the radio." He answered. He told us he must move on down the road. He wished us luck and said, "Drive safely and keep the shinny side up."

We climbed back in the cab, settled back into our positions, and I started driving. I knew Albuquerque, NM would be the next city large enough to have an electrical technician, who could fix our light problem. Therefore I settled back enjoying the cliffs off in the distance on both sides. It was interesting to see how the weather, rain, and wind had formed them so differently from one another. Some were straight up and others were hollowed out like big round caves.

Chapter 6

We arrived in Albuquerque in late afternoon. Dana went in the truck stop where all the phones were, to find a phone book. She was successful in finding an electrician, so we went back to the truck to wait for him to show up.

He drove up in an old, beat up pickup truck. His hair was long and in a ponytail. He did not appear to be a successful electrician, but in our predicament we would take what we could get.

We explained what the problem was and he jumped in the truck to make an assessment.

Meanwhile there was a man in a suit, which was not common attire out here, walking slowly towards us. He introduced himself as Jake and asked if he could by us some coffee.

We echoed, "Certainly" I don't think either one of us would have said yes if he hadn't been dressed in a suit.

The three of us went into the truck stop restaurant and sat in a comfortable booth. Jake began to explain that he doesn't normally do this, because he has a wonderful wife and two great children. However, he had some information about the truck we were driving, he would like to tell us for our own safety. He knew Fred, the owner of the truck we were driving. He explained that Fred is going broke, so he hadn't serviced or repaired his trucks in a long time. Jake knew this, as he had just hired a young driver, who quit driving Fred's truck and came to work for him.

Jake also is a friend of Bill, who said he had helped us on the road, and told Jake that we needed a CB radio.

Jake said, "I have a spare radio you can have for this truck. It will make your trip much safer. The drivers on the road can give you information over the CB, making your trip much easier."

"We sure would appreciate that," I said.

To which Jake answered, "Let's go to my truck and get it."

We gave it to the electrician and asked if he would put it in the space were the other one was pulled from.

He agreed, "It will make this job easier, but it will still take most of the night."

We went back into the diner to eat our evening meal. It was fun telling our story to Jake. His story was he had been a bookkeeper and couldn't stand to be locked up in an office from 9 to 5. When we finished eating, Jake offered to take us to a motel, since our truck wouldn't be ready until tomorrow. To our great surprise he then offered us a job with his company. He would be buying a new truck about the time we would be back in Los Angeles. We both were very happy to except the offer. We exchanged addresses and phone numbers. This was the most uplifting part of the whole trip. My idea of truck drivers has changed tremendously. It's just like any other group of people. It contains all kinds.

We both had a good night's sleep. In the morning we ate and then called a cab to take us to our truck. We were putting our suitcases in the truck, when the electrician walked over to us. He let us know his services took along time and cost Fred a lot.

He said, "Fred complained tremendously."

We thanked him and as he drove away I heard Dana say, "I am going to drive."

I said, "Wow, I am very glad to here this." I knew Dana pretty well, and I had expected that she would decide on her own time and then jump to it.

We climbed in and she started up the truck. While it was warming up, I pointed out the differences in this truck from the one we learned on. She pulled out of the truck stop. To enter the freeway she had to drive under the freeway, go one block then turn left, go one block again, then turn left, and then turn right onto the ramp of the freeway.

I was now the map-reader, who explained this all to her and then sat quietly. She moved through all the left turns just fine. To my unbelief, she tried to make the right turn from the right lane.

I yelled, "Move over to your left," It was to late. She was trapped with the cab up against a cement divider. She couldn't figure how to get out of there and said, "You take it out of here."

I said, "I'll get out and direct you."

To which she answered, "No, I can't do this."

"Yes you can and will, because I won't." I answered while jumping out of the truck.

I walked out into the second lane, held up my hands, and stopped all the cars that would be in our way.

She yelled, "You can't do that, get out of the road!"

Her voice began to break. She was trying not to cry.

I directed her to back up.

She was now crying and said, "I can't I'll be in the second lane."

"Do as I say right now or I'll walk off leaving you here" I yelled angrily.

She put it in reverse and moved back a little. She could then see it was going to work. I motioned for her to turn the wheel a little and keep going backwards some more. Then I gave her a stop signal, which she did. I ran over and jumped in my side. Then I directed her to turn left a little.

She said, "I'll have to go into the second lane to do that."

"If you don't you'll be in the same predicament you just backed out of." I said gruffly. "Just put on your left signal. Now drive left out into the second lane and then do a hard right, watching the back of the trailer in the mirror to make sure it goes around the curb and not over it."

She did this perfectly and we went up the ramp. As we came to the top, I told her to put her left signal on and slowly pull out into the freeway, while watching the traffic, too. I was relieved when she handled this perfectly. She stayed in the right lane for quit a while. I said nothing while just letting her get comfortable with the freeway. I felt it was necessary to tell her what the road ahead would be like.

I said. "When we go up ahead a ways, the road will change. It will become a two-way regular highway. There is a short set of small mountains and then it turns into another freeway on a straight mostly level road.

She said, "I didn't know about the mountains when I offered to drive, so will you please drive through the mountains?"

"Absolutely not, this is an excellent time for you to learn mountains and perfect the rest of your driving. Your doing fine here on the freeway. So relax if you can, and take what ever comes, when you see it. I'll be here to help." I said to her.

Soon we saw the signs warning the end of freeway is coming soon. Then we saw the signs ending the lanes one at a time. We were now on the small two-way mountain road. The first curve was manipulated very carefully and very well. Then there was a downgrade and an upward hill.

I spoke, "if you go faster down the hill you may have enough speed to get up the hill without down shifting."

She said quickly, "I'm going quite fast now."

"Look at your speedometer!" I said.

Surprised she said, "I'm only going 42 miles an hour, but it sounds so loud."

"Step on the gas and get going!" I yelled again,

She did speed up to about 50 miles an hour. We were about two-thirds the way up the hill. The revolutions per minute started to drop.

"I can't shift down," she said, "lugging the motor."

Then she did what everyone does when in trouble; she started to pull to the right. I jumped up on the doghouse and said, "Turn back to the left you're driving off the road. There is a huge drop down in a canyon on my side."

I grabbed the top of the wheel and pushed it to the left.

I said, " Now run the revolutions per minute up with the gas pedal and try to grab a gear."

She started crying again and said, "What one?"

"Any one you can get. Try for second or third." I said.

She slipped it in second, so we were going very slow about 15 miles an hour.   Neither of us had noticed how many cars and trucks were behind us. Some were even blowing their horns. I couldn't believe this big strong woman was crying like a baby. Soon we came to a place where there was a passing lane where everyone could pass.

Dana looked over at a passing truck driver and yelled, "He saw me crying."

"So what," I said, while she carried on.

We finally went over the top of the hill. She saw a small curve and a quite steep hill upward in the distance. She started going up through 14 gears as fast as she could. By doing this she was going faster than she had ever gone. She zipped over the top of the hill without having to down shift.

"Very good", I complimented her. She stopped crying and glanced over at me and said with anger in her voice, "If you ever tell anyone I cried, I'll hurt you very badly. Do you hear me?"

"Yes" I said as I started laughing.

Dana calmed down and was laughing with me. So this little mountain area is a perfect place to learn to down shift. On that next hill, when you get almost to the top let the revolutions per minute drift down. Then shift into neutral and with your right foot run the revolutions per minute back up to 2100 and shift into the next lowest gear. She did everything except grab seventh gear instead she grabbed sixth gear.

I said, "Alright, it doesn't matter that you went into sixth gear. It only matters you caught a high one and didn't have to go all the way down to second. Smile! You did it and you're not crying."

She said, "Thanks, I see what you mean about feeling more confident the more you drive."

We were coming to the prairie, which I knew she could handle.

So I said, "I'm going into the back and take a nap. If you need help call me. The road turned back into a freeway, so it should be easy from here to Tucumcari, NM.

I went into the back bed and fell asleep. I didn't expect to, considering the circumstances, but I had lost so much sleep in the last few days, that I was sleep deprived. I don't know how long I slept, and then I was awakened to a male voice saying, "Ya'll dropin at Philly".

Dana said, "Ya' where ya'll goin?"

To that I climbed in the front and said, "YA'LL, what is the matter with you?"

To which she said, "SSSHH, I'm talking to a trucker on the CB and that's the way they talk. She pushed a button, "This is Sassie Susie saying so'long, catch ya' on the flip."

Then she reached up and turned off the radio.

She said, "This is really fun and talking on the radio makes it more fun. These guys have a great sense of humor."

I was so glad to see her having fun. After that mountain episode, I was afraid she might want to quit. I know we both still have a lot to learn, but for now we both feel successful and are having fun.

Dana spoke up, "We are almost to Tucumcari. Jackrabbit said there is a Shell truck stop just as you get off the freeway on the right."

I spoke, "Great, this CB radio is definitely going to be a plus.

It's nice to have these freeways drop off whenever you come to a small town. We can run through town and stop easily to get what we need."

We filled the tank and she drove over in the truck line and parked. I jumped out and tied Bugsy to the trailer. We washed in the sink again, which was not fulfilling. I wish I could get into a shower and stay there for an hour. While we were eating we sort of made a plan to drive through most of the night. That is if we could do it safely.

While we were eating, Dana said, "We have a hurdle up ahead."

She added, "Some of the drivers on the radio said there is a weigh station open on our side in a few miles. It's the entrance to Texas, how do you think we should handle it?"

I spoke, "Now don't take this personal. But you can help us get through the first axle."

"Oh yah, and just how is that?" Dana mumbled.

"Well, ah, the first axle is about two hundred lbs over, so if you get out of the truck before we get right up to the scale, and run behind the weigh station to the woman's bathroom. You could pretend to pee and slowly come back out the other side of the station, and when I'm off the scales, run back to the truck."

"By that you're saying I am a two hundred pounder?" Dana said.

"No, but even close might help. Take you're purse with all the money in it and add the tire bumper to it. Come on do it for the team?" I said.

"O K, but I'll have you know, I don't weigh two hundred pounds." Spouted Dana.

"I've been thinking about this while I was driving. I am going to weigh the first axle, drive past the scales with the second axle as if I can't stop. When he tells me to back up. I'll struggle a little and tell him I can't get into reverse. I'll weigh the third axle, because the way we left these axles was the first was two hundred lbs off, the second axle is way too heavy, and the third was just right." I elaborated.

"What do you think, or do you have a better idea?" I asked.

She was silent for a few minutes and said, "I really haven't thought about it, and your idea is a stretch, however maybe we can pull it off, if you're a good enough actress."

We finished our meal and walked to the truck. Dana brought Bugsy into the cab. I checked everything on the truck and trailer extremely well. This was because we were headed for our first open weigh station. I drove her out on the freeway and brought my speed up to the Texas Limit. Pretty soon there was a sign reading "ENTERING TEXAS". A little ways farther was a sign that read, "DON'T MESS WITH TEXAS". We looked at each other, wondering what we had got ourselves into.

I asked, "Do you think we should still do our plan?"

Dana answered, "Well since it's your plan and not mine, I guess we should carry on."

"Oh Great! Does that mean you'll let me go to jail alone?" I said.

"Yes, cause someone has to be on the outside to bail you out." Dana said cockily.

"No kidding, what do you think they will do if they catch us?" I asked.

"The sign says, "Don't mess with Texas", and I have no idea what that means." Dana then asked, "Do you still want to do it?"

"To late we are going up the drive to the scales. So get out right now!" I said.

She jumped out and almost fell with her heavy purse. Then proceeded to go behind the weigh station. So I drove to the scales and stopped with only the first axel on it. When I saw the green light I started moving a little fast and stopped when the second axle had gone over the scales.

I heard a loud speaker come on and the weight agent yelled, "Back up and put your second axle on the scale!"

I fidgeted and wiggled the gearstick, and then fidgeted again.

I yelled out the window, " I can't get this darn truck in reverse."

He yelled back to say, "How long have you been driving this truck?"

I said, "Two years, but the gear stick has been acting strange for a while."

He hollered back to say, "Just calm down and put your foot on the clutch, shift into reverse."

I could see Dana peaking around the corner of the building. She was laughing at me.

I tried to do what he had said, but couldn't. I yelled back at him and said, "No matter what I do it won't go into reverse."

He said, "Go ahead and stop with the last axle on the scale."

Doing that was easy for me because I had a lot of practice on this particular thing in Ontario, CA, at the truck stop. So I moved forward and stopped with the last axle of the trailer on the scales. The light turned green, so I moved on to a place where I could stop for Dana. Dana came walking to the truck through her purse up into the truck and climbed in. As soon as she was in the seat I moved the truck out onto the freeway. Dana climbed on the doghouse and gave me a high five. Needless to say, we had a great laugh over that little stunt. After a little while of enjoying our successful, way of manipulating the scales illegally, we settled down and I concentrated on my driving. She was just getting adjusted to her bed and the dog.

When I said, "So you must weigh close to two hundred pounds."

"I do not so shut up and drive." Dana said with a chuckle.

Chapter 7

I was enjoying my driving time. Driving had always made me feel free and very relaxed. I imagined I could go anywhere at anytime.
It was still very cold outside and the wind blew straight across the highway. I could feel the wind push the truck and trailer to the left. This was unfortunate, because if a big burst of wind came along, I might not be able to control it, and it could push me over into the other lane. I held tightly onto the steering wheel, which was working for the time being.
I glanced up and saw the CB radio. I wondered how Dana had made it work.
I said quietly, "Dana, Dana are you awake?"
I heard not a word, I assumed she wasn't asleep, but didn't want to be bothered. So I reached up and turned a knob that looked like the turn on knob. The lights went on, so it looked like it was on, but there wasn't any noise coming out. Reaching for the

microphone, I put it close to my mouth and said, "Hello out there, can anyone hear me?"

There was along pause, so I repeated it. In a few minutes I heard,

"Kid are ya'll playing with Daddy's radio?"

I answered, "No, and I'm not a kid, I'm a full-grown woman".

"I'm very sorry, mum. Are you driving a truck?" The voice said.

"Yes, I sure am driving. This old red one going east." I answered.

"Well I'll be darn! What is your handle?" He asked.

"I don't have one yet, but I think it'll be Fender Bender." I said.

"What's yours?" I asked.

"Jack Rabbit," He said.

I told him I couldn't talk until the three trucks coming up behind me had passed me. I wasn't quit sure what to talk to him about anyway. The three trucks flew by and I heard him again.

"Fender Bender, are you still there?"

"Yes, I am." I said

"You must be right behind me. Can you see a blue truck, with a rabbit on the back right corner?" Jack Rabbit asked.

"Yes, so I am behind you. What do the truckers use these radios for, that is except for chatting?" I said.

Jack Rabbit answered, "We warn each other about on coming problems, like wrecks, roads being worked on, large holes in the road that usually appear in the spring, animals in the road, just general things that might cause trouble. We also warn about Smoky Bears. Do you catch my drift?"

I said, "Yes, but just how does that work?"

"Well suppose I saw an accident on the other side of the road. Later if I saw a truck going west over there I would call out, West bound Corn Flakes (nickname for Consolidated freight), there is an accident west bound, about a mile ahead of you. He would answer and thank me." Said Jack Rabbit.

"Now I know why everyone said we should have a radio. It would certainly help prevent accidents." I said. "It's starting to snow, so I'll drop back a little from you."

"By the way, how far do these radios reach?" I asked.

"It all depends on the radio, but the average range is about 2 or 3 miles." Jack Rabbit said.

"O K, I'll drop back just so I can still see you." Fender Bender said.

I did just that, as it was snowing harder and harder as we went along. We came into Amarillo, Texas. I noticed he was slowing down because the traffic was thickening.

We went all the way through the city and I heard him say, "Hey Fender Bender are ya'll still back there?"

"Yes I am and I'm getting quite concerned. The snow is blowing so hard, I can't see very well." I said.

I heard him say, "It's packin' up real tight and getting very slippery. So the best thing is to hang onto the steering wheel tight and don't make any unnecessary quick moves. Just continue on very straight at this slow speed."

I was getting very nervous when I heard him say, "You'll be comin' upon an accident.

There is an eighteen-wheeler in the ditch. Don't look at it, just go straight and steady."

I came upon the accident quickly, as the snow was blinding. The snow was blowing straight across the road, so I tried to stop looking at the snow and went carefully on my way looking at the line on the side of the road that was still visible. When I passed the accident, I said, "Hey Jack Rabbit, thanks for the warning."

We didn't talk much any more because it was too dangerous. We just drove what seemed like for hours.

 I heard Jack Rabbit say, "Now remain steady, cause you will be coming to a big accident on the other side of the road. Do just like you did before, steady and slow."

"Wow, I can see the lights. They are red, blue, yellow, and white glaring off the snow. It could be beautiful in the show like this, if you didn't know what was happening over there." I said.

I came closer and could see two huge trucks turned over they had crashed into each other. One was on fire. Plus there was a huge conglomeration of vehicles and people over there.

I was very nervous, I saw we had crossed the Oklahoma line, and I could also see a small sign saying truck stop next exit.

"Jack Rabbit, I've had enough. There is a small truck stop at the next exit. So I'm saying good-bye and thanks, and hope to talk to you again." I said to him.

Jack Rabbit answered, "I don't think you will like the truck stop, but it is safer than out here. Catch ya' on the flip." He was gone.

I took the off ramp and at the top there was a small arrow pointing left. So I turned and went on down to a farmhouse, just after which there was another arrow pointing towards a small country road, or more like a driveway. I went to the area that was slightly lit up. It was a fenced in square yard, with trucks all backed up to the fence so they were facing each other. I thought now I'll see just how well I've learned to back up. I found an empty spot and proceeded past it so I could do a ninety that was not on my blind side. Yes, I backed into the spot without any trouble, which I'm happy about cause all the trucks are parked so they can see me. I saw lights across the way flash on and then turn off.

I turned the motor off and rested there for a minute.

After a short while, another truck flashed his lights. Across the yard, the inside cab lights of a truck turned on and I could see a naked lady sitting up in the cab, putting on her clothes. She looked across the yard and saw some headlights flash on and off. When she was dressed, she climbed out of the truck and walked across the yard to the truck that had just flashed his lights.

I looked in the back of my cab, and shook Dana carefully. I had to shake her twice because she was really out.

I heard, "What?"

I said, "Be quiet! You have to see this. Get up here and for God's sake do not turn on any lights."

She came up front and saw some headlights flick off and on and she said, "Where in the hell are we?"

I said, "That's just where we are."

Some lights flashed across the yard and soon after, the woman went to the truck. She turned on the cab lights and undressed.

I could here Dana say, "Where on earth are we?"

I said, "Now watch! As soon as she finishes she will sit up in the cab with the lights on and dress."

Who ever wants her next will flash their lights and she will go there next. Dana watched her move to another truck and turn the lights on, to undress.

Dana said, "Now for real, just where are we?"

I said quietly, "We are in Oklahoma, but the reason we are in this truck stop is because the snow had turned into a blizzard. It packed on the roads and became very slippery. I had driven passed three trucks in accidents. One was on my side of the road and the other two were on the West bound side.

The accident on the West side was involving two eighteen-wheelers and some cars, I couldn't see what else. One truck was on fire and the rest were a tangled mess looking very ugly. Just after that, I saw a sign for this truck stop and decided to get off the road. I had no idea what I was getting into. I only knew what I was getting out of."

"Well this is certainly an entertaining truck stop. Too bad we are so tired we could stay up and watch the show. Did you walk the dog?" Dana asked.

"Are you kidding? She can pee in here, cause I'm absolutely not going out of this truck. I did feed her on the floor in front of the passenger seat." I said.

Dana said, "I'll take her out by the back of the truck."

Dana quietly opened the passenger door and slipped out with Bugsy. When they came back I asked if I could sleep in the back. I explained she had become such a professional toolbox balancer on the gas pedal we could both get some sleep. I also suggested we sleep feet to head giving us more room .

"When is the last time you washed your feet?" Dana said.

"The same time you washed yours, smart-ass." I answered.

She reluctantly said, "yes."

I was tired of the x-rated show, so I went in the back and putting my head on the passenger side of the bed, went fast asleep. I didn't even hear her come to bed.

Chapter 8

We woke up and noticed it was getting light. Dana opened the flap to look out. She called me up front. It looked like we were in a mud filled field. Most of the other drivers had left the field and in doing so they left big ruts in the mud. I was glad Dana offered to drive, because I thought she might be more likely to get out of here without getting stuck. She started the motor and to my surprise didn't check the truck before leaving. I guess she knew what I was thinking.

She said, "I'm not walking in the mud. As soon as we get to the first truck stop, we can eat breakfast and then I'll check the truck out."

I lay back down, to wait for breakfast.

We were in Oklahoma City, when she woke me. I was starving and I'm sure she was also. We grabbed our overnight bags and went straight to the ladies room.

"I tell ya', I have never felt so dirty in my life. Including emotional filth, after where we spent the night." I said.

Dana spoke, "You have to remember we weren't participating in the filth out there. We were innocent by-standers. We were trapped." Then she giggled and I joined her.

We cleaned up as well as we could in a sink. Dana said, "This a whore's bath."

I answered. "Not from what I saw last night." We giggled together again, and then went out to the restaurant. We found a far seat and it felt great to get out of the truck for a short while.

Suddenly I heard a chain rattling across the floor.

I said, "What in the world is that?" Then we saw Bugsy walking through the restaurant towards us. He came over to our booth; he was so big, his head rested on the table. I was hoping no one could smell him like I could. It was a combination of diesel fuel and dog smell.

Everyone was laughing except the waitress. She yelled, "Get that dog out of here."

I could hear Dana say, "I will, I will."

So Dana walked back through the restaurant with this big dog trying to sniff of everyone's meal. Actually one truck driver gave Bugsy some bacon. When Dana came back into the restaurant, the driver, who had given Bugsy some bacon, reached out and touched her arm.

He said, "Why don't you bring your friend and join us? My wife is craving some woman friendship and chatter."

She said, "We will be right there," and came to my table to ask if I wanted to change tables.

I said "Sure why not?"

We gathered our stuff and moved to their seat. They introduced themselves as Jim and Rosa. They were a driving man and wife team. We had heard of man and wife teams, but this was the first one we came across.

Rosa said, "How long have you two been driving?"

I answered, "We just started. This is our first trip, and what an eye opener it has been so far."

Rosa asked, "Why is that?"

Dana spoke up and shared with her, our experience at the last truck stop. When she finished, Jim wanted to know where it was?

To that Rosa spoke up to say, "We are not going to stay there, besides we have driven passed it. We have some trucking stories that will split your guts too."

"Oh, can we hear one?" I said.

"Well this one is personal, but very funny."

Dana and I both said, "Go ahead, what happened?"

Rosa began, "Well first I must ask you how do you pee?"

"Just like anyone else." Dana said.

"No I mean when your are in the truck. Because it takes too long to drive the truck off the highway, park in the line of trucks, and then go into the restaurant to do your thing. The male drivers will slow down on the highway and pull over as far as they can. The other man stands on the running board and pees on the side of the road, while the truck is still moving.

Jim doesn't want to drive into the truck stop every time I have to pee, so I had to figure a way to empty my bladder while we are moving." Explained Rosa.

Dana said, "We haven't come to that point yet. We are so late with this load it doesn't matter anymore. We just drive into a truck stop and go to the bathroom. However, we will have to learn how to pee while driving, as our next trip I'd like to be on time."

So Rosa started talking, "Well my solution is to have a coffee can, which I line with a plastic bag, in order to accomplish this feat. I have to set down in between the seats to do my thing. I'm lucky we have a conventional truck, which has the motor out in front of us. This gives me the space to pee were no one can see me. Just my head sticks up. Do you have a conventional cab?"

"No," I said, "so that will be a real problem for us. Does Jim have pictures of you peeing?"

She said, "He better not have one."

We were all laughing on and off during this discussion.

I said, "I can't believe we just met you and we are all discussing our different ways of peeing."(More laughter)

Rosa continued, "You must hear this. You probably don't know this yet, but when you back up to a dock to unload, you can't back all the way against it. You must stay a few feet from it, mainly because they may want the truck in a different place, which would be easier for them to unload in.

So one morning we were delivering in Los Angeles. Jim backed near the dock as usual and went in to ask the manager where he wanted the load. Meanwhile I had to pee. I took out my coffee can and plastic liner. I sat down between the seats on my pot, when another driver backing towards the dock and stopped even with our cab, so he could see my head."

We all were laughing at the table.

Then she said, "I waved at the driver and then seeing Jim in the rearview mirror, I signaled for him to come back to the cab. Jim began waving for me to drive the truck back to the dock, like I usually do. I looked at him again and waved frantically for him to come back to the cab. He again waved for me to back up the truck. So I reach up and sounded the air horn, which was deafening. Jim heard the horn, along with everyone else and came back to see what was the problem. The driver next door opened his window to ask if I was all right.

Jim said, "Yes she is fine," Looking at where Rosa was he started laughing and climbed into the driver's side so he could back the truck up to the dock. Now she could get off the pot without anyone seeing her, except Jim.

Rosa said, "I had a ring around my butt for two days."

We all broke into loud laughter.

"We must be on our way soon, but thank you for bringing us up to date on truck driving culture," said Dana.

Rosa said, "This has been very much fun. Everyone agreed. Then she asked where do you deliver?"

I answered, "Philadelphia and we are still a long way off."

She said, "To bad, cause we are going to Chicago, so we will be cutting north soon."

Dana said, "Yah, It would be fun to run along with you, but maybe we'll catch up with you two again sometime. What are your handles?"

Rosa answered, "We are Punch and Judy."

I said, "How cute, we are Fender Bender and Sassy Susie. Hope to run into you sometime again."

We all went to our respective trucks. Dana and I agreed if I drive, we would be on the schedule we made earlier. If I drive until about four or five o'clock, then she takes over and drives as long as she can without going to sleep. It is my turn next to wake up and drive as long as I can. Working out the driving times this way, maybe we can drive almost all of the night. We climbed into the cab and took our places. It was still cold out, but so warm in the truck, I felt lucky to be doing this for a living.

    I drove back out on highway forty again and went east. We had decided to take I-40 to I-81. I-81 makes a gentle curve up towards Pennsylvania.

Chapter 9

When Dana woke up, she came up to the front of the cab. We were having fun talking about our lunch with Punch and Judy.

Dana said, "We could pee in a pail."

"That's to big, I can imagine setting on a sharp edge pail and then you hit a bump, no, not a pail. How about a fruit jar, when finished we could screw the top back on." I said.

"We could try a plastic water bottle," Dana said.

"I'm not that skillful with my aim, let's just think about it for a while and the perfect container will come to mind." I said.

We both had improved our driving skills. Each of us had, by now, driven on many hills, where we could practice both down shifting and up shifting. I feel comfortable driving, and also sleeping behind Dana driving the truck, before dark. I know she feels very comfortable driving and loves to talk on the CB radio.

We drove through Arkansas and some of Tennessee. I stopped at a truck stop for lunch.

While we were still in the cab I said, "I would like to have a shower. Do you think I need one?"

"Yes, We both smell like pioneer women in a wagon train. I think we both should have a shower, but how are we going to do this?" Dana said.

Then she said, "I just thought of an idea. We'll take our bags in and one of us will ask the manager of the truck stop if we can take a shower in the men's bath room."

"I think both of us should approach him, and let him know we would like for one of us to shower, while the other one guards the door. Then we could switch positions." I said

Dana added, "We should be sure to let him know how much diesel we just bought."

So we tied up and fed Bugsy. Retrieving our bags from the outside storage space, we approached the truck stop. We walked slowly because neither of us wanted to talk to the manager. Once inside we looked for someone who looked like a manager. No such person was visible. We approached a young man.

I asked, "Could we speak to your manager?"

He answered, "I'll go find him for you." It took about five minutes to find him. They both came walking towards us. The manager looked to be about seven feet tall, which in itself was very intimidating. When they reached us Dana reached out her hand to the manager saying, "I'm Dana and this is Sandy my driving partner,"

He said, "Just call me Bill. How can I help you?"

I said, "Sir we have driven from California without a shower. Would it be possible for us to take a shower even though it is in the men's bathroom?"

Dana broke in, "We will take a shower while the other person watches the door so men can't come in."

I saw his face drop and I jumped in to say, "We will hurry and not put on makeup in the bathroom."

Dana jumped in, "We just bought three hundred dollars worth of diesel and will eat lunch after we shower."

He turned a little, rubbed his face with his hand and after hesitating he said. "OK, but do it fast."

We both smiled and thanked him and headed off to find the men's bathroom. There was a driver leaving as we walked up to the door. I reached for the door. He looked at me strangely and said, "Where are you going?

Dana answered, "She is going to take a shower. The manager gave us permission to shower in there?" He returned a quit nasty, "No."

Dana said, "Get in there quickly."

Is anyone else in there?" I said. It was silent so, I started in and then hesitated asking, "What about diseases most of these drivers probably have crabs or something worse."

Dana answered, "No self-respecting crab would jump off a warm body onto a cold shower wall. So go and quickly take your shower."

I went into the dirty men's room and checked out the showers. The one at the far end was the cleanest. I sat my clothes on a bench and turned on the shower. Grabbing the head, I made a circle with it, in hopes to wash off the one stupid crab that jumped onto the wall.

I could hear Dana arguing with some truckers, who wanted to use the bathroom. They tried to push her away from the door.

She yelled, "We have the manager's permission for us to use the showers. Now get out of here or I will call him in here."

Evidently they left because it was quiet again.

By that time I was in the shower and it felt so invigorating there, I stayed forever. I did take two showers and finished and dressed.

Dana opened the door and I went out as she went in.

She asked, "Did you find any crabs on the shower walls?"

I answered, "Yes, there was one dumb one so I washed him off."

She proceeded to go on in and I went out to stand by the door. It was quiet for a while, then two young guys came over to me and said excuse us, while reaching for the door handle.

I said, "You can't go in there, my driving partner is taking a shower."   They chuckled saying, "That's all right, we won't look at him."

"It's not a him. She is a women." I said.

One quite angrily man said, "Women shouldn't be in there and I have to pee now."

"The manager   gave us permission to take a shower." I said.

The other one said, "We just bought two hundred and fifty dollars worth of fuel."

I quickly jumped in to say, "We just bought three hundred and fifty dollars worth of fuel. So please let us be. We will be finished soon. They grumpily walked away.

Shortly another guy came over. He reached for the door handle.

I quickly said, " You won't want to go in there. Someone made a horrible mess. They over flowed the toilet on the floor and my husband is in there mopping and cleaning. By the time you eat it will be clean."

He said, "Thanks, I'll come back later."

As soon as he left the door opened and out came a clean Dana.

"Man, that felt wonderful." She said.

I said, "This truck driving makes one appreciate the very simplest every day things of life."

She agreed and we walked to the restaurant to eat. The last driver that had approached me at the bathroom door came over to our table.

He looked a little grumpy and said, "So this is your husband who was cleaning the bathroom."

Dana looked quizzical, "No, he is still cleaning."

The driver looked very embarrassed and said, "I'm very sorry." He went back to his table and never looked our way again.

I thanked Dana for covering for me. We ate and went back to the truck. I was feeling so clean and awake and ready to drive, almost like a regular human again. Dana climbed in with Bugsy and we were on our way again.

She said, "Before I pulled off the freeway a trucker going west warned me of another weigh station on our side that is open. He said it was a full scale, not an individual axle scale."

I asked, "Did he say how far ahead it is?"

He said, "It isn't very far ahead."

I began thinking of how we could get through the weigh station without getting a ticket. Dana was in bed and needed her sleep. I didn't want to get her up, so I decided to drive the front axle over the scale and stop with only the last four axles on it. I would try to convince him I couldn't back up again. We came to the weigh station and I pulled the front axle over the scale and stopped. Over the loud speaker the weight policeman asked me to back up.

I said, "I tried and I can't, there is something wrong with the gear stick."

He yelled, "Bring in your white slip."

I yelled back, "They are all white, which one do you want?"

"Your white slip, bring it in." He said over the loud speaker.

I yelled back, "I don't know what you want?"

He angrily said, "Pull your truck up to the parking spot on the right, and pull over and park it. Bring your white slip in here."

I heard Dana in the back say, "He wants your weight slip."

"Well why didn't he say so." I answered.

She spoke again, "He has a southern drawl, and so his weight slip sounds like white slip. Pull over and park, I'll go in with you."

I parked and took our metal notebook out of the door pocket. The two of us went shakily into the weight office. I could feel my heart beat fast because this felt like we had been called into the principal's office. We opened the door and went in.

He looked up to say, "To women? Where is the man?"

Dana said, "There isn't a man. We are the first all women driving team."

He looked down, shook his head and said, "Oh my God, What is this world coming to? Where is your white slip?"

I spoke up, "They are not white slips. They are weight slips. You didn't pronounce it correctly."

Dana grabbed me by the arm and pulled me behind her and said quietly,

"I'll take care of this. Just be quiet!"

She opened the notebook and took out five weight slips. Saying, "We had to adjust the weight a little, so there is more than one."

He again said, "Oh my God, I can't believe this. Five weight slips, with no time on them, so I can't tell which ones are the last ones. Let me see your driver's licenses."

We both took out our licenses, thinking we might be going to jail.

He looked at them and said, "Well I'll be damned. You really are professional drivers. Now take these five white slips and get on down the road. Also good luck with the rest of your trip you will need it."

I had all I could do to keep from correcting his white slip to weight slip again. We went out the door and almost ran back to the truck.

"Wow! That was close." Dana said. "I thought for sure we were going to jail or at least get a huge fine. Girl you better start learning when to shut your mouth and keep it shut."

"Yah, but he was in the wrong and it made me very mad. "So I defended myself.

She said, "You have to remember we aren't teachers anymore. We have no authority anymore. These weight agents
are cops and can dump us in the clink without batting an eye."

"Got your point, so go to bed," I said.

"That is exactly what I'm going to do, so don't wake me up again."

Everything was quiet, except for the motor. I was thinking, I can't believe this but I'm so used to hearing the motor now, it doesn't bother me anymore.

This road in Tennessee looks like it was built on a dyke. It was high, and then both sides drop off fast. In some places it looked like frozen rice paddies. I couldn't wait until summer to drive through here to see the rice paddies.

Chapter 10

I decided to turn on the CB radio. There was a lot of static and I heard someone say, "Hey eastbound do ya' have your ears on?"

I answered, "I'm guessing you're are asking if I have my radio on. Is that right?"

"Yah, ya' guessed it. Where are ya'll from?" He said.

"Michigan, but recently from California. Why do ya' ask?" I said.

"Ya'll sound much different from most of us out here." He said.

"Would you help me with some of this language used out here." I said.

"I would but I'm go'in west and will be out of hearin' range from ya' shortly. So I'll just say, "Catch ya' on the flip and keep the shinny side up." He was gone.

I began thinking about those two sayings. Keeping the shinny side up, of course means don't have an accident or tip over. I'm not sure of the other saying.

A truck flew around me going east. I said on the radio, "Got your ears on?"

He said, "I sure do sweetie? Where ya headed?" He said.

"Pennsylvania!" I shouted.

"Are ya'll new at this?" He said.

"How could you tell?" I asked back. "It's your tongue. It's quite different from most of us out here." He said. "What's your handle?"

"Fender Bender, so people won't want to drive close to me cause I'm new at this" I said, "What's yours?" I asked.

"Jumping Jack," He answered

"Speaking of my newness out here, would you consider explaining some of the sayings out here? I asked, like, "Bear in the air."

"Only a few, that is the sayings which will particularly help you while driving. Turn your radio to station four. We can talk there." Jumping Jack said.

So I switched my radio to four, when I heard him say, "Are ya' here Fender Bender?"

"Yes I am, so what does bear in the air mean?" I asked

"Think of Smokey Bear, he is a cop. Out here he could be called just Smokey, or just

Bear. So bear in the air means there is a cop in an airplane checking your speed. There will be white lines on the road, a mile apart. He times you from the first line to the last. He then figures out your speed. Soon you would come to a bear in the grass that would stop you and give you a ticket.

The drivers refer to money as green stamps. When a cop has you on the side of the road, you will here drivers say something like this, "How many green stamp are you coughing up?" explained Jumping Jack.

Since you are traveling east, the west bound trucks will warn you of bears, you will be coming up to a,

"Smokey in the grass at 56 mile marker, or bear in the ditch at 245 mile marker." Jumping Jack added. "Do you catch my drift?"

I answered, "I sure do, thanks for the help."

Jumping Jack said, "If you see a west bound truck you can ask him what's over his shoulder, to get some information about what you might be coming up on. You can also give him information about what is behind you so he will be safe also."

"Well I must say I feel much safer out here. This is my first trip and I had no idea what goes on out here. I think truckers were the first people to pay it forward, so to speak. It's a nice feeling to be part of this community." I said.

Jumping Jack asked, "Where is your partner, why didn't he explain all this to you?"

First of all my partner isn't a he. She is a woman. So you have just helped the first women driving team ever. I hope that doesn't bother you, cause we need all the friends we can get out here on the highway." I said.

"It certainly doesn't bother me. I think it's great. Maybe we can meet up in person some time. It was nice talking to a woman for a change and maybe soon this will all change for the better. Don't forget to change your channel back to 17. I'm going to head on out, cause I have to be in New York tomorrow."

"Catch Ya' later." Said jumping Jack and then he was gone.

Wow! He is going to be in New York tomorrow, I was thinking to myself. We certainly have some catching up to do. We should be driving about seventy miles an hour.

We shouldn't be going off the freeway so often and just simply speeding up everything we can.

After driving a while longer, I say a sign saying Knoxville is coming up soon.

The radio was coming in again and I heard someone say, "Hey east bound, beat up red truck. I'm sorry to call you that but I can't see the name of a company on your truck."

"It's OK, You got the Fender Bender here. Where are you?" I asked.

He shouted out, "I'm behind you I think, and my handle is Windy. I'm not sure if they call me Windy because I drive by fast enough to cause a big draft when I pass them or if it's because I talk too much."

"Well what ever, it doesn't matter I'll just call you Windy. Where are you headed?" I asked.

"I'm on my way to Charleston, NC. Have ya' ever been there?" Windy asked.

"No," I answered, "the reason we are out here doing this driving is to be able to see all of the United States, we possibly can."

"Well don't miss Charleston. It is a very beautiful town and a good time to see it is in the spring or summer." Windy added.

"We are delivering in Philadelphia. I suppose it is also very wintery up there." I said.

"Are you taking highway eighty-one north to Pennsylvania?" He asked.

"We are beginners, but looking at the map, we felt eighty-one highway would be the closes way." I said.

"Well as beginners, I'm guessing that you don't know about taking highway eleven from Knoxville to eighty-one." said Windy.

"As a matter of fact we don't know about highway eleven. Why should we do that?" I asked.

"Mainly because eighty-one isn't completed to Knoxville, so eleven runs you straight up to it. Actually straight isn't the correct word to describe it. It's a two-way small, curvy, and hilly road."

Windy said. "You go slow and be careful."

I thanked him for the information as he blew by us.

He said, "Did you know you have a flat tire on the inside left of your trailer?"

"No" I said as he interrupted, "There is a truck stop coming up shortly. Drive slowly and you can get there with no trouble, so they can change it."

"Thanks for letting us know. By the way your language has somewhat changed to a sort of Mid-western type." I said.

"You guessed it. I'm from Illinois. I'm going to cut off this highway soon and head a little south. So it was nice talking to you and I hope to catch up with you later." He said as he flew away.

"I'll say the same, bye." Said Fender Bender.

I heard a regular voice of Dana.

Windy said there is a truck stop up ahead that can fix this tire quickly. He also said it would be safe to drive slowly to the truck stop and nothing would happen.

She asked, "And just when do you plan to fix our flat?"

"I was waiting for you to wake up as you seem to deal with these men better than I do. That is, face to face." I answered.

"Have you even stopped and looked at it." Dana asked.

"No, but Windy said it will be fine until we get to the truck stop." I answered.

"Stop this truck on the side of the road, so we can check it ourselves." She demanded gruffly.

I pulled the truck over and thanked God there was room for us. I climbed down on the road and met Dana at the back trailer axle. From this vantage point, it looked fine. We looked at all of them and they all were looking good.

I said, "I'll go get the tire bumper."

When I came back I hit the first tire and that one sounded fine. The inside tire however, sounded like a very dull thud. So it was possible to tell it was flat by hitting it.

"Windy said there is a truck stop up ahead that can fix this tire quickly. He also said it would be safe to drive slowly to the truck stop and nothing would happen. That is mainly because the other tire will hold it up for a short while." I explained.

She said, "Well OK for now, but I have to talk to you about something. Lets get in the truck and off the side of the road."

I started the truck up and slowly pulled onto the road. Then I said, "What's the problem?"

She began to lecture, "Do you realize you are not friendly to these truckers?"

"Yes I am, I just haven't met anyone I would consider to date. Mostly they are unkempt and sometimes rude and even very sexually suggestive two minutes after you meet them." I answered.

"That is what truckers are like," She began, "We wanted to be truckers and that means we should be at least friendly to them. We definitely don't have to carry on with them, just be decent but firm."

"I guess I've not associated with people, who are like most of them, but I do want to be a trucker. However, being a trucker to me doesn't mean I have to be like them. I'm still myself no matter what." I answered.

Dana spoke up again, "I know, but we would both like to be helped on the road if need be, so it will be necessary to be friendly. I'm asking you not to stay in the truck when we get the tire fixed. Get out of the bed and talk to whoever is around, please."

"I'll try, but I'm afraid of some of them and others I like. However, you never know quite what you are getting." I answered.

We came to the truck stop. I pulled over by the garage door instead of by the diesel fuel pumps. I decided to stay in the truck while she talked to the mechanic about our flat tire.

He came over by my door and asked, "Will you pull it just part way into the garage so the back axle is just outside the door."

I placed the back axle just outside the door.

I started to move, while he went up in front of the truck to direct me where he wanted me to park. After I parked I climbed down from the cab and walked around the truck checking everything as I went. I felt someone breathing down my neck, so I moved away and saw a man standing very close, who looked similar to the one-toothed guy from school. My stomach turned, but remembering my lecture from Dana, I didn't walk away. I tried to think of something to say, while backing farther away from him.

I said, "Where are you from, sir?"

He said, "I'm not a sir. I was born in Indiana, but I haven't been home in years. I drive through there, but never stop."

To myself I thought I wonder why. Then he came so close I could smell him. It was almost like he was rotting inside and out. I bolted away again and happened to glance at the back of the truck to see Dana with her hand over her mouth trying to cover up a laugh. I walked on away again.

I heard him say, "Your blond hair is beautiful. Can I touch it?"

"Absolutely not," I answered.

Then he said, "I know what you want. Can I buy you dinner?"

To that I said, "No," while I scooted around to the driver's door and started to climb up, when I felt him grab my leg. I kicked his hand off and quickly jumped into the seat, and closed the door. He climbed on the first step.

Then said, "Don't ya'll get lonely up there?"

I could feel my anger swell up inside so I said, "NO I DON'T GET LONELY AND IF I DO I'LL GO TO HIM." Pointing to the dog, who by this time was setting on the doghouse staring at the stranger and sniffing loudly? " IF THAT DOESN'T WORK I'LL GO TO HER." I was pointing to Dana."

I said loudly and firmly, " Will you get down off my truck and leave now!"

Dana came walking up to my door. She was laughing so hard I thought she would fall over. She said, "I'm so sorry. I didn't mean for that to happen to you. From now on just talk to the ones who don't look and smell bad." Then she asked, "Did you really say you would go to the dog and if he didn't help, you would go to me?"

"Yes I did and I meant it." I said.

"Well, I see were I stand with you." She began to laugh again.

I began laughing, too.

Chapter 11

It took quite some time, getting our tire fixed and eating. I had a lot of time to think of what just happened. Now I felt sorry for him, as unpleasant as he was, just maybe it wasn't his fault. When I first saw him, my thoughts were what a lazy son of a gun he is. But maybe he had dysfunctional parents, who gave him no guidance of how to exist in this very hard world.

I heard Dana say, "I'll give you a penny for your thoughts."

I gave her a brief rendition of my thoughts.

She said, "Are you serious? What ever caused him to be annoying, and aggressive, and filthy doesn't matter. What matters is you didn't let him just take over you. You protected yourself just as you should. You actually showed him he shouldn't be aggressive with women. There soon will be more women out here driving and his lesson from you will help him."

I said, "I've always been a quiet person. Quiet is just how I am. However, some people interpret that as being stuck up, and snubbing people. I was thinking about that when you were lecturing me. So I decided to talk to everyone and anyone who came along. I obviously put myself in trouble with the derelict man."

She answered me, "I've never considered you as a snobby person and that's not what I was saying to you. I was trying to explain, just say a few words to some of these drivers, as we want to feel like part of the drivers community."

I answered, "I agree cause I felt much more comfortable and safer out here when I realized there is a sort of community among drivers. They have an attitude of I'll help you and you pay it forward existence." I also said, "I just hope he is all right because I didn't want to hurt him. I was simply not letting him hurt me."

Dana added, "I think he was too drunk to feel hurt. I'll walk Bugsy and we can get out of here."

"Sounds good to me," I said. I went to the outside storage compartment to get my pajamas. Searching through this compartment I came across an ice bucket, we lifted from a motel, and suddenly it hit me. This would be perfect for our pee container. We could get some plastic bags, which would fit it and our pee problem is solved. I motioned to Dana to show her I would be in the truck stop store. I didn't know if they carried plastic bags, but went in anyway. They not only had some, they had a perfect size. I bought them and meet up with Dana at the truck.

I said, "Guess what? I found the perfect thing to pee in."

She asked, "What is it?"
I held it up and said; "This motel ice bucket and I found the perfect size plastic bags for it in the truck stop store."

She thought a minute and then said, "Yah, I think the ice bucket will work. Let's get in and go. I'll drive and you can pee."

To which I answered, "Smarty!"

I sat in the passenger seat and grabbed the map saying, "Jumping Jack said we would have to take highway eleven up to interstate eighty-one. Interstate eighty-one isn't finished all the way down here. I'll guide you to highway eleven. Go back the same way we came in here and look for Broadway, which turns into highway eleven. Turn right on that highway. Give yourself room the make a right turn."

From that statement I received a very dirty look. There was a pause and
then I said, "He also said the roadway is sort of
mountainous, as we will be coming into the Appalachian Mountains."

Dana said, "I feel much better about driving in hills. I've been practicing on the smaller ones we have gone through."

I said, "I noticed your driving has improved very much. This highway is a small two-way highway. With this slight bit of snow, it might also be slippery."

I said, "I'll sit up in the passenger seat for a while to assist you by answering the radio."

"That will be a help, I appreciate it." She said.

"I looked on the map and highway eleven is only about sixty miles or so." I added.

"There's Broadway where we should turn right." I said.

Dana pulled a little into the fast lane and made a perfect right turn. I am sure glad she is smart. When Broadway turned into highway down to a two-way road. Dana appeared quite comfortable, except "He also said the roadway is sort of hilly and curvy.

I then noticed Dana was swinging her head back and forth.

I asked, "Would you like a solution for glancing back and forth from one outside mirror to the other outside mirror." She was busy and quiet.

I asked her again, "Did any of your driving teachers explain to you how to stay in a lane, without glancing back and forth from one mirror to the other."

Her answer was no.

So I asked if I could show her.

She said, "Absolutely, any time you see where you can enhance my driving, or make it easier, please do."

"I would like you to do the same for me. I know without a doubt you learned more from those books than I did. Your scores tell the story." I said.

"Anyway, back to the mirrors, if you look into the mirror on your side of the truck you can see where the middle line is, compared to the truck. Move the truck about one foot from that line. Now glance at the right mirror to see if the right side of the truck is a small distance from the edge of the road. Now look straight ahead to see where the line in the middle of the road comes up on your dash, if it is extended with your eyes and imagination." I explained. "So as long as you keep the middle line of the road, on the dash in the same spot it was when you was one foot from the center line, you will know the truck is placed correctly on the road."

Dana played with the information I had just showed her and said, "Wow, this works a whole lot better. Thanks and I'm glad we can help each other out without a lot of hurt feelings. We make a good team and we will be successful, you wait and see."

"OK let's get through this supposedly difficult road," I said.

For a while it was quiet. I thought how beautiful this would be in spring, summer, and fall. The rolling hills where not only beautiful, but fun to ride through. Trees were mostly deciduas with a few pine trees thrown in along the road.

Then I heard the radio static and said, "You got the Fender bender east bound."

"You got the Ruff Rider here to tell you the road looks pretty good ahead of ya'. The snow will stop a few miles down the road. How's it over your shoulder?"

"It's snowing but the road is pretty well cleaned off." I answered.

"I thank ya'll, catch ya' on the flip." He said and then was gone. Both Dana and I noticed the traffic was getting much lighter because of the holiday.

That meant we could breathe a little easier, but still be careful. Bugsy was also relaxed lying on the doghouse between us.

A voice came over the radio, "You've got Santa west bound. Ya' got your ears on the little red truck?"

"We sure do. You have a pretty clear road ahead with a small amount of snow melting." I said.

He said, "Ya'll have an eighteen wheeler on the side a mile up. He can't get all the way off the road because there isn't much shoulder. His motor quit and there will be a wrecker soon to pick him up. Therefore, all you have to worry about is getting beyond him. The traffic is light so it probably won't be a problem."

"Thanks for the info, talk to ya'll later." I answered.

Neither of us spoke, we were trying to anticipate what we would be coming up to. Soon we could see it on the down slope of a hill and wouldn't you know it, there was a west bounder on the down slope of the next hill coming toward us. Dana started to slow down, and then we heard a voice on the CB say, "You go around him first and then I will."

We just slipped out into the other lane and went by the crippled truck. A second later the westbound truck came shooting by us.

I said on the radio, "Thanks west bounder, and thank god for these radios."

Dana said, "I thought the radio would help, but mostly to warn us of cops. But now I have just seen how it can save our lives. We will have the thank Jake for giving us the CB."

Dana was doing great going up and down these hills. They weren't like the ones out west. They were much less of a degree tilt and shorter. So you don't have the possibility of gaining much speed and going on forever.

Dana said, "I see a sign for I-81. Yippee! We will soon be on a big freeway."

"That's good news." I said.

Once we were on the freeway, I felt relieved and proud. It seems like every bump in the road we come to, we've climbed over. Maybe not very graceful, but we get it done. I expect the grace will come with experience.

I sat in the passenger seat because there is something I would like to ask Dana. I haven't been able to ask her, because it's very personal. Oh well, I'm going to go for it.

"Dana." I said, "There is something extremely personal I would like to ask you."

"Yes, Sandy. Since you already know way more about me than you need to know, I can't imagine what else there is for you to know." Dana said.

"Uh um ah I know you do this because I sleep behind you, however I can't do it and I very much need to." I explained. "When I'm driving for a while, I have pains because I mainly can't hold the seat down, when I have to pass gas, the seat is so tight to me that when I lift up the seat comes up, too. It pushes everything back up into me. Once I put my hand on the edge of the seat to hold it down and "wham" it smacked me really hard when my hand slipped off of it." I looked over at her and she was trying not to laugh. All of a sudden her laughter exploded and brought mine out along with it. I let our laughter settle down and said, "Come on tell me."

She said, "So you want to know how to fart while driving." We both laughed again.

"Yes, I do." I said.

Dana reached over to take a newspaper out of the door pocket. It was all folded up small and neat. She held it next to her right thigh, did a quick jump up and shoved it under her right thigh and then farted.

So that's why you were so upset when I through the news paper out in Knoxville?" I said chuckling, "Here I thought you, as an intellectual, wanted to read the paper, but all you really wanted to do is fart."

After we stopped laughing I said, "On that note I'm going to bed."

She said, "OK, you go back to pee and I'll stay up here and fart."

I can't believe just four months ago, we were up in front of a classroom as teachers, being very proper and classy and now listen to us. This proves it is hard to go up in status, but one can fall quickly into the depths of talking truck trash. I went back to sleep.

Chapter 12

I don't know how long I slept, but when Dana asked me to wake up, I finally felt like I had a good sound sleep. I dressed and went up into the front seat. It was dark outside, but very beautiful. The snow had accumulated on the pines, and shone beautifully in the moonlight.

"This is beautiful. Where are we?" I asked.

Dana answered, "Virginia, in the Appalachian Mountains. According to a trucker I was talking to, there is a nice truck stop up ahead on the right. I'm feeling tired so I think we should stop there."

"Sounds fine to me." I said.

She pulled down the exit ramp and into a nice paved yard. Dana went over to the left and pulled into a row of trucks, which was a straight ahead shot. I took Bugsy's leash and climbed down to walk him a little. He was being the best dog on this trip. I was thankful for that. By the time I came back Dana had fallen asleep with her head resting on the steering wheel. After tying Bugsy up, I woke her up and we proceeded to the truck stop.

Wow! What a neat place. There was a Teletype with instant news coming out of it.

This was great, because with the CB radio on all of the time, we couldn't get the news from the regular radio. I like to know what is happening in the world. Next there was an elegant red leather barber's chair surrounded with thick glass. The full time barber was setting in a smaller chair reading a book. We walked through this area to a hallway.

As we walked down the hallway,

Dana said, "Look at these guns on the wall. Some of these are antiques. They are encased in glassed in frames. What a wonderful collection of guns. Look! The whole wall is full of them."

"This is a truck stop to remember. At the end of the wall was a huge clock which tells the time all around the world." I said amazed at all of these decorations.

At the end of the hall we walked into a nice restaurant turned around and saw a sign over a big wooden carved door. The sign read, "Professional drivers only."

I pointed it out to Dana, who headed straight towards it, with me right behind her. She opened the hand carved beautiful door, and we went in. As soon as the waitress saw us she yelled across the restaurant to say, "You can't eat in here, this is for professional drivers only. Didn't you read the sign over the door?"

Dana spoke, "Yes we saw the sign and then came in because we are professional drivers."

"I don't believe it. Are both of you drivers?" She asked.

"Yes we are. Now can we eat?" I asked.

"No, I want to see your licenses." She said kind of grumpily.

"I'll go out and get them. Sit down and rest." I said to Dana. So Dana sat down, but only for a moment, cause the waitress told her to go back out the door.

It took me about five minutes to find the licenses and log books. When I came in again I was amazed all over again, this place was wonderful. Dana was standing near the wooden door. We opened it and went straight over to the waitress and spread our papers out on the counter. The waitress examined our papers and then said angrily, "Are you whores?"

A neat looking driver spoke up to say, "That wasn't necessary. Now please feed these women."

We thanked the driver who spoke up for us. Then we went to the nearest booth. It had brown leather seats and was very soft and comfortable. Soon the waitress brought a small loaf of fresh baked bread and the menu, which had several homemade meals listed on it. The bread smelled so good, I tore off a piece and buttered it. It tasted as good as it smelled.

I said to Dana, "I think we have died and gone to heaven."

She answered, "Yes, what a trip. We went both to hell and heaven."

The driver who had stood up for us a while ago, turned around to say, "I'm sorry for listening to your conversation, but I couldn't help hearing you say that you had been to hell. Does that mean you drove through Gallup, NM?"

"Yes we did." Dana spoke up, "But I didn't see anything similar to hell there."

The driver spoke again, "Did you drive through in the daytime or at night?"

We both said, "Daytime."

"Well, that's why. You should drive through at night especially on a Saturday night. There is an on going feud between the truckers and the Indians. The Indians talk on the truckers CB channel and blab on and on. This makes the truckers mad, so they drive very slowly to clog up the main street of town. The last time I went through I was stopped at the one and only stop light. There was a very drunk Indian trying to cross the street. He was weaving all over, the light changed to green, but I couldn't go because by now he was in front of my truck. So I put my head out the window and asked him to hurry up. He just gave me the finger and stayed where he was. A few minutes went by, so I blew my air horn. He sat down in the street, in front of me, to take off his boots. He stood up with a boot in his hand and proceeded to bust my left light out. He wobbled over to my right light and broke it out also. He then just sat down and put his boots on, and went on his way. I had to stop at the end of town to buy two new headlights. The Indians are so poor I didn't want to press charges, I just went on my way."

"That's quite a story," I said, "Now I'll know never go through Gallop at night. How long have you two been driving?"

"About five years," He said, "and you two, how long have you been driving?"

Dana answered, "This is our first trip."

"Oh my word, how did you learn to drive?"

Dana said, "We went to trucking school in Los Angeles and just about failed it, however we passed our driving test, so here we are."

One fellow stood up and wanted to shake our hand. He was on his way to Boston. He wished us luck although, he didn't think we would need it. We thanked them for helping us and making our trip much more pleasant.

Their words made me feel proud of what we had accomplished. It meant much more coming from Truckers.

I ordered a meatloaf dinner and Dana ordered a beef roast dinner. They both came with huge pile of mashed potatoes tinted with garlic and filled with gravy. There was a great sample of vegetables. Our taste buds haven't been so happy in a long time. It was quiet while we ate. I was taking in the moment and once again trucking has made me appreciate one of the simple things of life to a great extent.

After a while Dana spoke up, "Mine was delicious how was yours?"

I swallowed and said, "The same! I love this place. Someday I want to sit in the big red barber's chair and get my hair."

Dana said, "The barber probable only knows how to cut a man's hair."

"I don't care, with the wave I have, in a couple weeks it will be fine." I said.

Unfortunately, we had to leave this truck stop and head out to Philadelphia. Walking out we went slowly to take a better look at the decorated walls. There was also a collection of antique knifes. We walked past the barber's chair and on out into the cold winter night. As much as we hated to leave this oasis, it was necessary. Dana climbed in back with Bugsy; I took the driver's seat. I went up the driveway and onto the freeway.

This freeway was in perfect condition, with no bumps and it had bright lines; it looked as though it had just been built. There was some snow falling, however not enough to make the roads slippery. The meal I had just eaten helped to energize me. I settled in to keep my speed up and practice down shifting and also some up shifting.

Chapter 13

I had covered much ground and it was beginning to get light. I've heard just before dawn is the hardest time to stay awake and I absolutely believe it.

I started waking up Dana. She groaned and moved around a little.

"I need some help up here. I'd like you to be in on a decision we have to make." I added.

"I'll be up there just as soon as I am dressed." Dana said.

Bugsy came up in front, so I knew Dana would soon follow. I could hear her wiggling and moving around. She was struggling quite a bit.

When she arrived in the passenger seat she explained, "The space in the bed area isn't big enough to dress in. First of all you have to set up on the bed to dress. This position is almost impossible to dress in."

"You could come up front and set in the passenger seat to dress." I said.

"Every trucker on the road would be talking about it on the CB radio." She said, "No thanks, because they would flash their lights and you know what flashing lights mean."

"Yes, I also know just what you think of dressing in the front, so not a good idea." I answered her.

"I wanted to talk to you about the fact that we are coming up to a toll freeway. I know Fred asked us not to take toll roads. However it is the shortest, fastest, and safest way to Philadelphia from here." I reported.

She wanted to look at the map, so I handed it to her. After she studied it for a while she said, "I agree with you. How far ahead is it?"

I answered, "It is about fifty miles away. I woke you early as I am at times starting to fall asleep. Plus, we should get some change ready. Could you do that please?"

"Yes I will. The money is in the back, so here I go again." She said. "Do you know how much the toll is?"

"No, but just get all the money out, so we'll be ready." I said.

Dana climbed in the back and then yelled out, "Don't you think it will be just some sort of change if I put our change in a box, that should be enough."

I answered, "Yes I think so, but bring the rest of the money out here, just in case it isn't enough."

In a few minutes she was up in the front of the truck and had the money organized and ready to pay. The traffic slowed way down, because of people trying to pay tolls. So we both sat there waiting, a sign became visible, which gave the toll amounts. Dana was fiddling with the money to make sure the correct amount was in the box.

The traffic was so slow it was stop and go. During one of the stop intervals, I happened to look down at the floor of the cab. I saw a knob and was wondering what it was for.

So I asked Dana, "Do you remember when you read the book on this truck and pointed out all the knobs and their purposes?

Dana said, "Yes, why?"

The traffic moved a little more and we were finally two trucks from the pay station.

I said, "There is a knob on the floor over here by my seat and I don't know what it is for? Do you?"

She said, "No and if it was in the book I would have remembered it."

I asked, "While we are stopped here should I push it?"

She answered, "Sure why not?"

I reached down and pushed it and nothing happened. So I pulled it, and all of a sudden all of the air went out of my seat. The seat went down to the floor, so I was sitting on the floor of the cab. I started laughing uncontrollably. All I could see was straight forward, the clutch, the brake, and the gas.

I couldn't see out either the front or side windows. Dana was laughing also until she saw the truck in front of us move forward.

She jumped up on the doghouse and yelled, "Put the clutch in, now give it a little gas, OK put on the brake and hold the clutch in. Keep the clutch in and the brake pushed. I will run the steering wheel and the gear stick and tell you when to push one of those three pedals. We were still intermittently giggling.

The truck in front of us moved, so we had to move up to the pay booth.

She yelled, "Take your foot off the brake and push in the clutch." She shifted into first gear and yelled, "Give it a little gas." She steered it to the pay bucket, which was a big wide container so you could drive by and through your money in. She picked the moneybox up and reached over my head to toss the contents of the box into the money bin. I could hear the money clang on the metal and then we were through the pay gate. We were moving very slow. I could feel her turn the steering wheel to the right To which I said, "What are you do doing, we can't drive all the way to Philadelphia like this!"

She yelled to say, "I'm crossing three lanes of traffic to the right side of these lanes, where there is a parking space. Push the brakes, now, put the clutch in." To that we stopped.

She said loudly, "Hold the clutch in and give it a little gas, now!"

As I did that we were already in first, so the truck moved forward and she turned the wheel to the right. We move like this for a short time.

She said, "STOP, push the brakes in, push the clutch in and turn off the key."

"I can't reach the key." I said frantically because I had no idea where it was from where I was sitting.

She reached down to the key and said, "I got it."

Thank God the truck turned off. I looked up at her to see her laughing which turned my laughter into an uncontrollable amount of laughter and crying. I couldn't stop. She was in the same condition. She climbed back over to the passenger seat, jumped out, and came over to my side of the truck. She opened my door and seeing me sitting on the floor, way below the steering wheel and the windows, just cracked her up again I then jumped down from my position to the ground. I still couldn't stop laughing and crying at the same time. A trucker walked over to us. So we both asked if there was a bathroom nearby. He pointed to a small building, to which we both took off on a dead run to the bathroom.

After we went to the bathroom, we put cold water on our faces. My stomach hurt from laughing so much. We soon gathered ourselves up and headed for the truck. As we approached the truck we could see the trucker, who guided us to the bathroom, was still standing by the truck. He motioned for us to come over by the driver's seat.

When we arrived, He said, "I want to show you something." We both watched as he put his thumb on the knob and pushed down on it. The seat went slowly back up to the correct driving position. I didn't think I could laugh anymore, but it just came out again. Of course Dana joined in.

Once things calmed down a little, Curt introduced himself to us. He asked where we were delivering our load?

Dana answered, "Philadelphia, we have four drops there."

Curt said, "Wow, that's a difficult city to deliver in, and four drops is a lot. Who gave you this load?"

I answered, "Fred Stenger, we were looking for a job, as a two women team, and he had this job going out on Christmas Eve, which his other driver wouldn't take. So he offered it to us if we would take it out

Christmas Eve Night. We jumped at it because we had been looking for a job for two months."

Curt said, "If you like, we could grab a bite at the first stop on the toll road. It's only about five miles from here. I've lived here all my life, so I can give you tips on how to drive to your delivers."

"Thanks, that would be awesome, since this is our first trip we can use all the help we can get." I said.

He said, "Let's get going. Bring your bill of laden into the restaurant. See you there.

"We both said, "Bye"

We all climbed in our respective trucks and took the ramp towards Philadelphia. At the toll road stop, we brought into the restaurant our bill of laden, which had all of our drops and their addresses. As we ate he wrote instructions of how to get to each delivery. We explained to Curt how much this would help us and we were extremely appreciative of his time and help. He admitted there was many things he couldn't help us with, but he felt we would be able to work them out.

He said with tongue and check implications, "However knowing all the trouble you had with the air compression knob on your driver's seat, I'm not all sure you can handle them."

We all had a big laugh visualizing me in the seat on the floor. We finished our meal, and it was time to say good-bye and thanks again. Dana and I went on our way, filled with anxiety and excitement of our very first drop in Philadelphia, PA.

There still were a couple of hours driving time, so I went into the back of the cab to get some sleep. I had asked Dana to wake me when we get close to the Gulph Mills exit.

Chapter 14

It felt like I had just laid down when I heard, "Get up, we are almost there."

I moved around and noticed that my skin was sore. I should have put my pajamas on, but was too tired. We had discovered if you have levies on and leave them on, while both sleeping and driving, you will have sore skin where the seams of the levies hit your legs. This is because there is a slight jiggle constantly, so the minuscule movement of the seam on your leg rubs it until it is sore.

I climbed up into the front of the cab and sat in the passenger seat. I could see a sign for the Gulph Mills exit.

I said, "Once you get off, make a left and go under the overpass. We will be going north on the highway. Go until it changes to highway Amaline Drive. We should see our delivery place on the left.

Curt said This is an easy delivery.

"Do you want me to do it?" I asked.

"No, I'll go up to let them know we are here." Dana said.

She pulled to the back of the building, where we could see the dock. She stopped the truck and walked up onto the dock. I moved over to the drivers seat. There were already two trucks backed up to the dock unloading. She came back to tell me I could park over between some swing sets and the garbage cans.

Dana climbed into the passenger seat to say, "The manager said we have to wait until one of these trucks leave to make room for us to back in. So wait in your truck."

Dana said also, "Those drivers are unloading their trucks themselves. They are complaining about it, so they are working very slowly to anger the man."

"We have to unload it after driving all the way from Los Angeles." I complained.

"Yes, and he laughed hysterically after he said it." Dana added.

Dana said, "I think we should unload and act like we are happy about it. That way he will compare us to the men who are unloading now, and think we are excellent drivers. Besides only a quarter of our load comes off here, not the whole load."

"Maybe I should lay down again, as I'm very tired." I said and then climbed into the back. Before I slept I was thinking that Curt had said this is a straight backup to the dock. However, this man has us parked in a position that would cause us to do a blind ninety to get to the dock. When it is my turn I will backup a long way so I can pull in again and make a left turn and go until I am straight out from the dock. It will be a straight shot back to the dock. I won't tell Dana because she will want me to back in from where we are, but since she isn't the one backing up, I'll do it my way. Now I could sleep.

After two and a half hours, one of the trucks pulled out, so Dana walked over to ask if we could back in.

The manager said, "No, not yet because, the driver who is still here is afraid we will hit his truck."

Dana said, "We are excellent drivers. Let us show you. My friend can put our truck on a dime, if need be, so please let us unload. We have three more loads to drop before New Years."

"Well," said the manager, "If someone gave you a load with four drops, I guess they had great confidence in you, so go ahead and back up."

After Dana explained what had just happened, I started the truck up. I backed all the way out. Dana and the manager were waving their arms frantically, but I totally ignored them and pulled the truck in again and did a left turn, so the truck was straight out from the empty stall. Now all I had to do is back straight up, which I did, being careful not to touch a thing. I stopped near the dock and slowly backed up to the dock. I climbed out to see they were clapping for me. I must say it felt nice.

I went up on the dock to get ready to unload. They brought out a forklift and asked if we knew how to use it.

"Of course not, No dock manager has ever asked us unload." I said.

A man came out with a forklift. He demonstrated how to use it, which was very simple and kind of fun. The manager said we had to bring the materials to the back of the trailer and put it on the forklift. His men would be responsible from that point.

We started unloading, but sometimes it would take both of us to lift the huge boxes.

"How are we going to know where to stop?" Dana asked the manager.

"All our boxes are labeled BDLC, there should only be twenty-five boxes for us."

I whispered to Dana, "Thank God."

It wasn't long before we were done. The other two drivers were still unloading.

This first drop was like a great success, but I knew they wouldn't all be like this, so I just wanted to take this first unloading job into my head and I wanted to savor the moment.

We walked towards the cab, smiling to ourselves. I climbed in the drivers seat to pull the truck forward far enough to let Dana get in. I pulled out of the loading spot so we could look at Curt's directions again. It appeared the second drop would be a small distance in the country from Philadelphia. Dana pointed out on the map a shorter way through the city to the main road we could take to the second drop.

I said, "I don't think we should take the short cut, mainly because Curt directed us this way for a good reason. From my experience driving in the eastern cities, I've learned the old bridges are sometimes to low for today's trucks. They also won't hold a truck this heavy."

"I could get out and walk over the bridge." Said Dana with tongue and cheek smile.

"OK, I'm sorry, if asking you to walk around the chicken coop bothered you, but it worked. I thank you for doing it." I said.

"Chicken coop, where did you learn that?" Dana asked.

"I was talking to a driver on the CB and he explained many of the terms the drivers use. He said they call the weigh stations, chicken coops." I said.

"Let's take Curt's route and get moving." I said.

Dana agreed, so I started driving. The road was quite small, with tall trees lining it. I again, could imagine how beautiful this would be in the summer. I am sure I'm noticing this because I have been out west for a while and

I miss the Michigan tree lined roads. We came to a very confusing situation we've never seen before. It was a screened in protection for people waiting for the streetcar or bus. The weird part was a driveway around the back of the screened in bench. Neither of us knew if it was proper to drive behind the screened in bench or in front of it. The first one I came to I drove behind it.

 I said, "I think these strange drive- ways are for cars dropping off people for the street cars or busses. Therefore, I am going to drive straight on the street."

Drive straight through is exactly what I did and nothing happened to us, and this being the last one we saw, surprisingly we didn't get into any trouble. We kept going on Curt's directions. The thing we noticed about these inner city streets was their size. They were small compared to inner city streets out west. I use the method Joe had taught me. This kept my truck directly in the middle of the lane. After a while we were out in the country. The roads were bigger and driving was easy. Seventy-five miles later we saw the building, which was our delivery point. It was a storage building with a huge yard in front for delivery manipulation. There were no other trucks in the yard, so I asked Dana if she wanted to try this drop.

"Sure, why not. Given an acre to turn around in, is my style of drops." She said.

I put the break on and got out to talk to the manager.

"Where would you like us to pull up to the dock?" I asked.

He said, "Have him put it in that last stall next to the wall."

I corrected him "The driver isn't a him, it's a her."

"Then you better have her put it out in the middle so she won't hit anything," He said.

"She won't hit anything, so if you want it on the end she will put it on the end." I said grumpily.

"I asked you to put it in the middle, so put it in the middle, now. While I call my nephews to come and unload it." He said.

I walked over to Dana, who was now in the driver's seat.

"Put it in the middle bay. That is number five." I explained to her.

"I'm checking with you, I should drive in a circle and when I come to number five, make a sharp right turn, so I can drive straight out from five?" She asked.

"That will do it just fine, then do your favorite thing, back straight up to the dock. I'll be up there to tell you when to stop." I answered.

She did it absolutely correct, except for a little bump of the dock. I thought to myself Dana is a good driver; it's just her confidents need lifting. Probably the fact these men watch us with every move we make and never think we can drive just as well as a man can, doesn't make it easy to do these manipulations in front of them. I'm confident we will get accustomed to their watchful eyes and grumpy mouths and in the end we will be excellent drivers because of it.

No sooner did we get set for the unloading, then two boys about fourteen and sixteen years old came running up on the dock to unload. They did a fine, quick job and soon where done. We thanked them, closed the doors, and went on our way. We had seen a small country truck stop on our way up here, we went there to eat and plan our next drop.

Chapter 15

We drove to the truck stop. The snow and rain had softened the ground, which was not paved. It was filled with deep ruts and sloppy mud. I'm beginning to see how easily trucks just go through mud and makes it's own ruts, so it was not a problem, which I had thought might be. We parked in the first row. Other truck stops have several rows of trucks, but this one was easy to get into with its two rows. We went to the bathroom to clean up.

Dana said, "A shower would feel so refreshing, but there isn't one here. We should get a motel when we are fully unloaded, which should be tomorrow."

I added, "I agree, this being a holiday weekend, will give us two days in a motel. We must have a tub, so I can soak, and soak, and soak. Then sleep, and sleep, and sleep. You can sleep, and sleep, and sleep. Then soak, and soak, and soak."

"Yes, but I'm going to fight you for who soaks first." She said, "We'll see but for now let's plan our third delivery. Curt indicated this drop would be the most difficult one." I said.

It is on a steep hill. We must enter on the road at the top of the hill. We must drive down the hill and stop past the driveway, then backup and make a ninety-degree turn into the driveway. He said there is very little room in the yard, so depending on which dock they want you on and how many other trucks are docked already, it could be difficult to get in there.

"It's late and there is a difficult drop tomorrow, so I suggest we stay here tonight, even though it is difficult to sleep in the cab." Dana said.

"Maybe we should switch sides in the bed and also see if we can figure a better way to hold the gas pedal down, so it will stay down all night. Maybe we can tie it to something?" I suggested.

"I'm going out to check the two little storage closets for something that will work." I added.

I looked in the closet on the driver's side first. There was a huge chain and a hook, but I didn't see how either of those would work. The passenger side closet looked a bit more promising. There was a smaller chain, a hammer, some tools, and some metal hand weights. I took the hand weights over to the driver's side. I opened the cab door but stayed on the ground so the gas pedal was more visible and easier to get to. There was a metal rod, which came out of the floor of the cab. It went downward towards the gas pedal and then bent in an "L" shape up and connected to the pedal. What luck, as one of these weights should fit into the curved part of the rod? The thirty-pound weight fit. The larger ends helped to keep it from sliding off either side of the rod. I added some tape on both sides of the weight to make sure it held tight. Dana came out and grabbed the dog to take him for a walk.

    I finished taping the weight down when Dana came back, "Great fix! I hope it holds all night, cause we both can use a lot of sleep." Dana said. "By the way do we have an alarm clock?" she added.

"Yes, I have a small one in my extra pack in the overhead space." I answered.

"Should we get up about seven o'clock?" I asked.

"Sounds fine, cause we are going to sleep now, which is about eight pm. That is eleven hours sleep, which sounds fantastic to me." Dana said.

"I think Bugsy is comfortable with us now, so he should be fine out in one of the seats or on the doghouse." I said.

She agreed, so we all settled down for a long winter's night.

At about midnight a knock came on the side of the cab. We both jumped up and sat staring at each other wondering who in the world would be out there? Then a much stronger knock, scared us both until we heard a feminine voice say, "Would ya'll like a date?"

Without delay Dana said, "Get lost bitch, I'm working this row!"

We both lay down and were giggling again, but quietly. What had just happened seemed very much like a dream. It didn't take us long to fall back to sleep.

We woke up before the alarm and went into the restaurant to eat and wash up. We then went on our way to the third drop.

At the top of the hill I took a deep breath, then started down the hill slowly. The weight of the truck was pushing the cab, when I took my foot off the brake. I chose granny gear, so it would help keep the truck from running away on this hill. I stopped with the trailer a short distance from the driveway. This was a busy street. People started yelling and blowing horns. One car stopped directly in back of me, so I couldn't back up.

"Will you get out and go ask the driver in back of me to go around me?" I asked Dana.

She did and stayed in view of my mirror, giving me directions.

One man shouted at us, "Get that damn truck out of the road!"

To which Dana said, "Shut up and go around." He and two other cars went around.

Now I could back up, but when I took my foot off the break, the truck started forward, so I quickly put my foot back on the brake. I had to put it in reverse, quickly take my foot off the brake and put it on the gas. At the same time turn the wheel to the right so the trailer would turn into the driveway. Once I was in a short distance, Dana waved at me to stop. Part of the cab was still in the road, so all the commotion started again. In this position, facing the road, I could scream back at them, give fingers back, and what ever else I could think of. The one comment they made that infuriated me was, "You should let a man drive that truck, since you can't seem to do it."

I was perspiring terribly, as this was quite pressuring.

Dana came back and said, "There are two trucks in back of you, and just to their right is an open slot. That is where he wants you to park."

I climbed out of the truck and walked around it. This looked to be an impossible task. Also to the right of my truck was a hill or a pile of dirt, which is where the employees of this company parked their cars. I climbed back in the cab. The only way I could do this is to shut out all the yelling and horns and concentrate on the job of slowly moving this huge truck into the parking spot by the dock. That is exactly what I did. I turned the wheel to the left, which would direct the trailer into the beginning of the parking spot.

"STOP! STOP!" Shouted Dana.

So I did and called her up to explain what was wrong.

"That is the correct way to turn the wheel to maneuver into the spot, but the cab then goes straight toward the cars parked on the hill when the truck jackknifes." Dana said.

I climbed out to look at it again, because the mirror was of no use with the cab turned in the opposite direction. I could see I would have to go back and forth a few times, making adjustments each time, to slowly guide the trailer into the parking spot.

"I asked Dana to yell at me when ever the cab came close to a car. Then I could pull forward again and readjust it so I wouldn't hit the car and the trailer would go a little farther into the correct spot."

By this time the dockworkers became aware of the situation and came out to supervise. One person stood in front of his car to keep me from hitting it. Fortunately, I had already passed his car, and I knew with just a couple more adjustments I would have the truck parked. I kept on working and finally the trailer slipped into the spot, with the cab following it.

I had to calm down and wipe myself off with a towel.

As Dana walked by to go to the dock, she said, "Wow, what a good job. I'm going to buy you a drink for the great blind ninety you just did. Joe would have been proud of you."

She went on her way up to the dock to observe the unloading of goods.

I was feeling all kinds of emotions, however, the best were accomplishment and success.

Chapter 16

After we were unloaded, the other trucks were already finished and left the dock. This made pulling out of the dock a whole lot easier than backing into it. I drove out onto the road and a short distance from the driveway; I stopped at a little restaurant with a truck parking lot. We took a clean set of clothes in and washed up in the sink again.

Back at the table, we ordered our food and looked at Curt's directions again. We could see we had to travel through residential areas to get to the industrial park, which is where our last drop was located. I had to relax quite substantially, before I could attempt to drive again.

Dana said, "We can't stay here to long, as we both have agreed that we would like to get this load completely off the truck before New Years Day, which is tomorrow."

I said, "I know, I'll need about another half an hour, and I'll be ready to drive again."

The time flew by and we climbed into the truck again. Following the directions, I turned left and from that point on, Dana would read the directions to me. There were several streets we had to drive on. Some were small and some were nice and wide.

Soon we came into the industrial park, and to my surprise it was beautiful. There were tall trees lining the paved pathways. Many grass lawns all around the designed factory buildings and warehouses.

We found the correct address and proceeded on a long paved winding driveway. At the point where the driveway ran into the docking area, there was a huge boulder on each side of the driveway. These were obviously to prevent drivers from driving their trucks on the beautiful grass lawns. As I came to the docking area, I could see the docks on the left and the driving area extended way out to the right of me. I thought this is perfect, cause I can swing to the left at first and cut to the right, which should put the truck in a perfect position with the end of the trailer facing the dock. This would make it very easy to back straight up against the dock.

So I started this procedure and ended up just as I thought I would. I waited here ready to back up, when we get permission to do so.

Dana jumped down and walked across the paved lot to the office. It had begun to rain unusually hard, so Dana was running and jumping puddles. She went into the office, which had large windows, so I could see Dana and the manager pointing and shaking their hands. I saw the manager point directly at our truck. After a short time, Dana came out of the office and stomped over to me sitting in the truck.

She said, "He is very mad at us."

I asked, "Why?"

"Because of the rock under the truck." She said.

"Well pick it up and through it out of the way!" I ordered.

"I can't cause it's as big as a refrigerator." She shouted.

"Oh my gosh, where is it?" I said

She said, "Get down here and see for yourself."

I jumped down and walked to the back of the truck, only to see one of those huge boulders, which had been at the corner of the drive, was now in front of the back wheels of the trailer. I started to laugh, I couldn't help it, and so I covered my mouth with my hand. I heard Dana snicker, also. The strange thing is I hadn't felt the truck pull the rock at all.

Dana said, "The manager said we have to back around the boulder and leave. We can come back after New Years to unload."

"You're kidding, he won't unload us because of the rock?" I asked.

"No, he was very angry about the rock, plus he had already let some of his workers go early because of the holiday." She explained.

I walked back to the front of the truck, climbed into the drivers seat and sat for a minute deciding how to get around this boulder. I cranked the steering wheel hard to the right, which directed the cab out around the boulder, when I backed up the truck. Now I could pull forward pulling the back wheels out from around the boulder. This lot was so big I could pull forward making a complete u turn and head toward the driveway. At this point I stopped and waited for Dana to get in. there weren't any other trucks, so we sat there figuring out what do and where to go, as we now had two days before we could finish delivering. The rain was getting extremely heavy, and water was running in little streams on the driveways.

    We knew we had to find a motel, which had a large parking lot.

Chapter 17

 I remembered a sign for a motel with truck parking on the second road back. We decided to look for that one mainly because we where not at all familiar with this area. Also, I didn't think it was too far back. By now the rain was pouring so heavily it was difficult to see where I was going.

 Finally we came to the road, which the motel should be on. It was much wider and easier to maneuver on. There were two lanes going my way and by this time the water on the street was so deep, I couldn't see the curb. Suddenly the traffic came to a halt. I hit the brakes to slow way down. There was no obvious reason for the stoppage. I could see the freeway bridge we had to drive under and there didn't seem to be any accidents in front of us. We were creeping so slow we were almost stopped. It would have better if we were stopped, because my leg wouldn't be hurting so much from holding down and letting up on the clutch. The overpass was a long block away. I had the truck in granny rear. Still I had to push the clutch in to slow down and let it out to speed up again. It took forty-five minutes just to get to the overpass. There was a huge puddle under it.

I said, "Dana, would you please turn on the CB radio, to find out what is happening up front to cause this traffic jam."

She turned it on and we could here a lot of drivers cussing.

We heard a driver say, "Wow what a mess! I can see three eighteen wheelers and who knows how many cars in a huge accident?"

The next voice said, "Where is it?"

The first voice said, "It's on the seventy-sixth freeway westbound.

The second voice again, "It's probably because, not only is it pouring rain, but also, this is a holiday weekend, so everyone in Philadelphia and all the suburbs around it are trying to get out of town for the holiday."

The first voice, "I made a big error, by getting off the freeway onto highway twenty-nine, not realizing the cops have directed all the westbound traffic onto this highway. I think that is because they can go down to two hundred and two and go westbound again.

This traffic is so slow, my truck won't go this slow, so I have to stop and start over and over."

I said, "That is the exact description of the way I have to drive."

"That truck way up ahead is the on the CB." Dana said.

"You are probably right." I said.

With the rain continually pouring down and the streets filling up with water, it was becoming a somewhat scary situation; mainly because you couldn't tell what lane you were in. By now my left leg was throbbing from clutching and letting up on the clutch. This clutch wasn't your usual car type. It was very huge and quite hard to push in. I had to some times just stop and let the cars in front move on. After an hour and a half, I could see the motel, which had been advertized, as having truck parking, on the sign.

I said, "Dana the motel up there, is one more block on the other side of the road and it is the one with truck parking."

Dana said, "Sandy, would you like me to drive?"

I answered, "There is no way to change, because of those three cops directing traffic up there. Thanks anyway."

So I hung in there and was now rubbing my

leg trying to keep the muscles from being so tight. I could feel a knot between my knee and ankle. I realized we had to drive a half block and another full block to make a left turn to get to the motel. It took forty-five minutes to get to the last block. I saw a sign, which read left turns make the next right.

I asked, "Dana did you see that sign?"

She answered, "Yes, it's a half circle, which will direct us around, to cross this part of the street we are on, so we can then turn left on the other side."

We came to the circle, so I turned right and about half way in the circle, a policeman came running at us, while blowing his whistle, and waving his arms. I stopped immediately.

I asked Dana, "Did I do something wrong?"

She quickly said, "No, not that I could see."

The water, where the policeman was running, was over his ankles. He made his way to my door, which he hit with his fist, while yelling, "WHY DIDN"T YOU STOP AT THE ORANGE CONE?"

"What orange cone?" I asked.

"The one at the beginning of this turn out. Do you think I put it there for exercise in the rain?" He said.

"There wasn't a cone when I turned in here." I yelled.

Dana jumped out her side, getting all wet, so I knew she was walking back to see if there was a cone.

The young cop asked loudly, "Do you do this for a living?"

"Yes, Do you do that for a living?" I asked, "Standing out in the rain getting all wet?"

He furiously yelled, "Let me see your drivers license and your papers?"

"They are in the log book in the other door pocket. I'll climb over and get them." I said.

While I was doing that, I heard him say, "You should keep them in a better place closer to the driver."

Hunting for the papers I mumbled under my breath, "You stupid ass."

He asked, "What did you say?"

"Nothing." I said.

"You did too, I heard something." He said.

"You're hearing things," I said and then mumbled, "You stupid ass." Again, with my head bent down.

"WHAT WAS THAT, YOU JUST SAID?" He yelled.

"I didn't say anything and here are my

papers." I answered.

He asked, "Do you have any tickets on this license?"

"Not a one," I answered.

"Well I can fix that; one for illegal parking, one for ignoring road signs and I'll think of another reason." He said.

"I heard that," said Dana, now standing beside him, "Plus there is not a cone in the road. There is a cone in a yard way over there floating in a pool of water."

By now he was so angry, he threw my papers down in the water and said, "You drive out of here and turn right back into the road you came from. Do not make a left turn!"

"I have to make a left turn, because my left leg is killing me from pushing in and out on the clutch so much." I explained.

"He said, "You cannot turn left. Have you got that?"

"Yes, then I'll just stay here until the traffic thins out." I said.

He yelled again, "You will move out of here and turn right or I'll get a tow truck in here to tow you away."

"And just how will you do that, by helicopter?" I respond.

Dana picked up my papers from the water and climbed in the truck.

She quietly said to me, "Tell him we will move and turn right to get out of here."

I did what she said. He said, "Good, get going!"

Because I didn't want to go to jail, I followed his orders with much anger inside me. I pulled a right turn into the right lane of the same road we had been on. The pain in my leg replaced some of my anger. I drove on for a while and I saw an answer to getting out of this bind. Up ahead there was a funeral home with a circular drive in the front. I didn't say a word to Dana cause she might say no. I just pulled into the funeral home and went around the circle drive.

Dana yelled, "What are you doing?"
I answered, "Making a left turn out of here."
I heard her mumble. "OH, my God."
I quickly said, "It's ok. This will work."

I slowly drove through the circular drive. Some bushes where scratching the trailer side and a tree scratched the roof.

So I followed an old Michigan rule when in doubt speed up. I moved forward through the drive to the road. Then out into the street a little, so cars knew I wanted to cross the street. They were traveling so slow they didn't seem to mind letting me through. I went on through, put my blinkers on and turned left. As I pulled into the right lane on the other side of this road, we both breathed a sigh of relief.

We soon came upon the cross street where the three policeman were standing. As we passed them I blew the air horn and waved.

Dana said, "He was laughing."

I said, "I sure hope so, I was quite frightened when I realized he wanted to take my license away, or I should say give me three tickets so I couldn't drive. What a creep!"

"He was young and probably in training." Said Dana.

"Well anyway, we should hide this truck at the motel."

"You have to be kidding, no one can hide an eighteen-wheeler." She stated.

"We can park it in an unrevealing place, like somewhere behind the motel," I said.

We came to the motel and I turned into the driveway. Dana went in and found us a room with a bathtub. I was lucky to find a parking spot directly behind the motel. We didn't hear anything from the police after that.

I enjoyed this motel like I've never enjoyed a motel before. We both did. Free from problems and cops. I love trucking, but this trip was so long and pressuring, I needed a break. I soaked in the tub and then fell asleep for ten hours. Dana awoke a little earlier and took Bugsy out for a walk.

She came back and said, "There is a cute restaurant just a short walk from here. So wake up and lets go eat."

While we were eating I asked Dana, "Do you think Jake was sincere when he offered us a job?"

"Yes, I thought he was an honest man." She answered.

"What do you think of calling him to see if he still has a job for us."

"That is a good idea. Let's call him when we get back to the motel." She said.

After we ate, we walked back to the motel and just did nothing for a while. Dana found the phone number and dialed Jake. Jake answered the phone, thank goodness he was there and not out trucking. Dana chatted with him and asked the question. I saw her smile and say a loud, "YES!"

With that expression, I knew he still had a

job for us. I was so relieved and happy at the same time. I love trucking, even if it makes me appreciate the smaller things in life in a very literal way.

Chapter 18

The day of our last drop soon came. We woke up early and walked to the restaurant for breakfast. We discussed how we both felt a little uneasy facing the dock manager. He had been so angry about the "Rock", that it was a bit alarming to us.

I said, "I sure hope he doesn't want us to put it back in place."

We began to laugh.

Dana said, "The rock looked so funny in the middle of the parking area, I couldn't help laughing."

Back at the motel, we packed and walked way out in back to our truck. Dana and I were anxious to get back in. However, Bugsy had a look on his face that said do I really have to get back in that thing.

I petted him and lifted him up so he could jump up into the seat. I went over to the drivers seat and climbed in. We just had to back track to the industrial area. We drove up the driveway for the second time. There it lay, like a huge dinosaur egg, right in the middle of the parking space. I drove around it and lined the truck up again, with the dock.

Dana said, "Well here I go. Wish me luck."

She jumped down and crossed the lot. Dana talked to the manager and came back to the truck, with a smile on her face.

"He wants you to back up to the dock and don't hit anything." She said.

At this point we were both ready to bust into laughter, but trying very hard not to. It might infuriate the manager and we didn't want his scorn again.

I backed straight up to the dock and didn't hit a thing, mainly because there wasn't anything to hit. Dana went up on the dock to watch the unloading.

After an hour went by and we saw a forklift go down a ramp from the dock, at the other end. It chugged, chugged, and chugged slowly over to the rock. The forklift pushed its forks under the boulder in the lot and lifted it. I looked in the rear view mirror at Dana. She had her hand over her mouth so they couldn't see her laughing. This view cracked me up. Thank goodness I was in the truck where no one could see me laugh.

Once the forklift had put the rock in its proper place, it chugged back up the ramp and went out of site. We waited another half an hour and someone finally came out to unload us.

It seemed like a long time to unload, but we didn't care because once we were finished with this load, we would be on our way to pick-up another load back to Los Angeles.

Two hours later they had finished unloading our first load. We gave each other high fives, jumped up and down, and yelled we've finished our first cross-country load.

We decided to back track to the freeway and instead of going under it, we would get up on it. This would be our best chance of finding a truck stop. Once on the freeway, Dana was on the CB radio asking truckers were a truck stop might be, on our side of the highway. A trucker came on the CB and said we will be running into one about five miles at Wilson exit.

I drove up the exit and saw the truck stop. I parked in the line of trucks at the truck stop. There was great excitement in the truck, Bugsy was exited, but of course he had no idea what for.

Inside the truck stop, we went to the wall of

phones. Dana picked one up and dialed our dispatcher. She gave him our location, so they could find a load back to Los Angeles. The dispatcher warned Dana the east is the most difficult place to find a load out of. He explained, because of all the large cities and huge population, it is easy to take a load to the east. However, this brings a large number of trucks in the area looking for loads out. He said he would call us back when he found a load for us, but it might take a day or two.

This news was not what we wanted to hear. The waiting game had started. We filled some of our time with business. Thank goodness this truck stop had a laundry mat on the grounds. We also completed our logbooks, so they were accurate. We read up on the news and finally the phone call, we had been waiting for came.

I think Dana likes to talk more than I do, because she always runs to answer the phone first. I was standing by her and saw her face drop. My thoughts were, 'not another disappointment.' When she finished her call, I asked, "Now what could make you look so disappointed?"

Two truckers also using the phones informed us some information about this pick-up.

Supposedly, it is a high paying load, but picking it up is a difficult task. To pick it up, one must drive backwards down a small lane, with a fence on one side and trucks backed into the dock on the other. When you come to an open space, it is necessary to do a blind ninety, to back up to the dock.

We both were concerned, however, I didn't think it could be any harder than the load we had dropped at the company on the hill.

After the truckers left, Dana told me the real bad news. Our load was going to a small city south of Huntsville, Alabama.

She explained she had requested Los Angeles, but the dispatcher said there were no loads to Los Angeles. It was either sit still or go to Huntsville. So we are going near Huntsville.

My geography wasn't very accurate in the east, as I immediately thought New Jersey was a long way off. I looked at the map and could see I was wrong. Using the scale on the map it was approximately one hundred miles. In trucker's eyes, this is an excellent trip. We went into the restaurant to eat and figure out the best way to travel to the coffee pick-up. It was on the New Jersey shore of the Atlantic Ocean. Knowing this made me excited to see a new place in my country.

    After lunch, we climbed into the truck. I was driving and she was reading maps. This has worked out for us because I like to drive and crowded places don't bother me anymore. Dana on the other hand is happy to read the map in these situations. Most of our travel to the New Jersey coastline was on freeways. After we drove off the freeway, it was a short jaunt to the coffee distributer building.

    I parked beside the road, next to a field. We both jumped down from the truck and walked down the driveway towards the ocean. There was a large freighter docked out on the ocean side of the building. It had "Columbia" written on the side of it. I don't know why this affected me so, in a positive way. I felt like a successful citizen of my country, doing my part to keep things in order, transporting goods and helping the economy work. I used to read about this in geography. Now I am carrying coffee, which came from Columbia, to a state that needs it. In reality I know teaching is a much more valuable occupation for my country, but you almost never see your results.

    Dana went into the office to talk to the manager, while I walked out to the ocean.

There wasn't a beach; it was all dock, with the boat tied securely to the dock. I could see the people from South America walking on the boat. I wanted to talk to them, but couldn't and even if I could reach them, I didn't speak their language. I walked back to the truck. I took Bugsy out in the field next to the truck.

Dana came back to say, "We will have to wait until a spot on the dock opens up. The manager said there is a small coffee shop out by the roadside in this building, where we can wait and eat. There is a loud speaker in the restaurant he will use, to let us know when it is our turn.

The day went by and no call from the manager. We will spend one more night in this truck. It wasn't too bad since we've learned how to keep the gas pedal down all night, and knowing that Jake's new truck for us, had a double bed, was incentive enough for us to handle this again.

We woke as the sun came through the front windows. Breakfast in this restaurant was great, especially the coffee. No sooner had we read the paper, than we were called over the loud speaker, and the call said to go to the last stall on the dock.

When I had walked down to the ocean, I didn't pay attention to what the last dock looked like. However, if there were nothing on the far side, like a wall, it would be much easier to back up to the dock because we would have more room to maneuver.

I started backing down the small driveway. I backed past nine trucks. The last spot was next. I stopped the truck, climbed down to take a closer look at where I had to park this truck. Thank goodness, there was five feet past the spot. This would make backing up to the dock easy. Back in the truck, I turned the wheel clockwise causing the trailer to turn towards the dock. I went as far as I could with the back wheels of the trailer on the five extra feet. I turned the wheel the other way and drove straight out to the fence. With one more clockwise twist going backwards and one more pull forward, I could back up putting the rear of the trailer up against the dock. Done!

Chapter 19

The three trucks closest to ours had left, so getting out was a matter of simply driving forward. Since it was early afternoon, after I took the truck out of the parking place I stopped so Dana could drive. I helped her get on the freeway, so I could lie down without worrying. I wasn't worried about her driving just finding the correct freeway as several freeways crisscrossed this area.

I didn't realize how tired I was, but I fell off to sleep immediately. I'm sure Dana was having a great time talking to truckers, as this area has thousands of trucks running around.

Dana drove to Johnson Ville, Tennessee. This was the longest she had ever driven. I'm so glad she is really getting into this cause it takes a lot of pressure off me.

I was sick to my stomach, causing us to stop for the night. We did our usual setup with the gas pedal, and had our usual bad sleep in these conditions.

We woke as the sun came up, and I said, "Won't trucking be so much more fun and better for our health, when we have Jake's new truck?"

Dana answered, "Yes, I can hardly wait. We will have a queen size bed. There will be closets inside and out and best of all, we won't have to tape the gas pedal down."

Needless to say, "I'm very much looking forward to the new truck, too. Did the dispatcher say we could get our next load to Los Angeles?"

Dana answered, "He wouldn't promise, but said he would try to get us home next trip."

We ate and as usual worked out the trip to our next drop. Huntsville was close enough for me to drive the whole thing, letting Dana have a rest.

Approaching the area of our drop, I don't understand why, but I was unusually concerned about this drop, the backing up to the dock, that is.

I expressed this to Dana, who said, "We have plenty of time, so why don't we drive to the coffee distributer to check it out?"

"Sounds like a winner to me." I answered.

There was a little map on our bill of laden, which we followed. The street to the drop was small, and with every block became narrower. This district looked like a deprived economic area.

The houses were actually falling apart and they needed much repair. I saw one house boarded up. The real strange thing was, there were no people. I keep driving slowly because the road was, at this point, very narrow. The trees were very tall and shaded the whole area. It began to mist, making this whole scene very eerie. I slowed way down. The farther we went the worse and even intimidating this place looked. Still not a person was visible. The road was now about five feet higher than the shoulders. The edges of the road dropped into wet swampy ditches. The road was so narrow it was hard to keep both front wheels on the pavement. We came to the last crossroad and just beyond this road was a locked fence. The fence had been locked so long, that vines had almost covered it up. I stopped before the crossroad, so we could decide what was best to do.

"Well this is a mess! Now what should we

do?" Said Dana.

"I'm not sure, I'd like to try turning right, because the real gate looks to be two streets to our right." I said.

We could just barely see the huge distribution building through the vines on the fence.

I started to turn right on the last crossroad. I move the cab to the right, but the left back wheels of the trailer, slipped off the pavement. In fact a small portion of the road broke off.

I jumped down to look at the back trailer wheels. They had also swing to the left and had slipped down off the road enough so the trailer was leaning towards the ditch.

"Now what?" I questioned.

Dana was speechless. This situation looked hopeless to both of us.

I said, "What would you think of calling a wrecker to hook onto the trailer and pull it back on the road."

Just as I finished talking, three vicious looking dogs came running towards us. We both climbed up into the cab. The dogs looked diseased, they were full of ticks and fleas, and had worms crawling out their buts.

I said, "What next, I expect to see the army

come down the road in a tank shooting at us."

"I can't believe this." Dana said.

Thank goodness we could both laugh at this. We both just laughed it all out. When we calmed down, we came back to, now what should we do?

The outside dogs hadn't left, because they discovered Bugsy in the cab. We now had four dogs barking at the top of their lungs and still no sight of any people.

I had a hard time convincing Dana she must go find a phone because she was bigger than I. She wanted to take Bugsy with her, but I said, "NO!"

"Bugsy can't stand up to those three dogs, besides he will get diseases." She reluctantly agreed, jumped down and then picked up a board and swung it yelled, "GET OUT OF HERE. GET, GET OUT OF HERE!"

They ran a short distance, and every time they came towards her she yelled again.

Eventually they lost interest and wondered away. Dana continued on to find a phone.

It seemed like a very long time before Dana came back.

She said, "A wrecker will be here when he finishes transporting a damaged car to a repair garage."

I said, "Lets go check out the gate up ahead, maybe it will open."

Dana asked, "What good will that do? We can't go in there, that would be breaking and entering."

I said, "If we can open the gate and the wrecker is able to slide the trailer back upon the road, we could drive straight in, turn around and come back out and leave. That is the only way we can get this truck and trailer out of here. It won't go around these corners without either the cab or trailer falling into one of these ditches."

We walked towards the gate, discussing this solution. Reaching the gate was another blow to our plan. The gate had a huge pad lock on it. I began pulling some of the vines from the gate so we could get a better look at the lock. It was rusted, however, on very secure.

Back in the truck, we were quiet, thinking of what to do next and hoping the wrecker would be able to slide the trailer upon the road again.

Bugsy began to bark, so we knew the wrecker was behind us. A driver Jumped down from the wrecker parked behind us.

The young man was walking toward us and

said, "How on earth did you do this?" He began to chuckle and we laughed, too.

He said, "Just what is it you want me to do?"

I said, "Do you think you can hook up to the back of the trailer and pull it back up on the road?"

He said, "I can certainly try, but in order to do that I'll have to drive down in that lawn, as he pointed to the right.

Dana said, "We've been here for at least two hours and haven't seen a person, plus that house is boarded up."

He said, "I'll drive down there." He did just that. He swung a big chain from the back of the wrecker and hooked it under the trailer, back by the last axle.

He looked up at us and said, "Wish me luck!"

He started the wrecker and began to pull. At first there was no movement of the trailer. He put it in another gear and pulled harder. The trailer slide a little, so only one wheel was off the pavement. The second wheel caught on the pavement instead of sliding over it. Now the front of the wrecker started to lift up in the air, instead of sliding the trailer over any farther.

The wrecker was way up on its back wheels. The driver lowered the wrecker very slowly. Thank goodness the trailer stayed where it had been pulled.

"What is your name?" I asked the driver.

He said, "Ed." Then I introduced us.

Ed said, "Wow, that was a first. My wrecker has never lifted up like that before."

I said, "I hope it will be all right?"

"Definitely," Ed said, "but I don't think I helped you much."

"If you will do one more thing for us I believe we will be able to get out." I said.

Dana asked, "Do you have a file for filing metal?"

"I'll look." He said.

I said to Dana, "I'm going to straighten the truck out."

In the cab, I turned the wheel a little to the left. Slowly I backed up and the cab went back into the intersection. I quickly turned the wheel to the right and went forward slowly until the whole truck and trailer where in a straight line facing the gate.

Dana said, "Good job!"

I answered, "Thanks, I've been thinking about this for quite a while. I'm certainly glad it worked."

While Ed was gone we agreed if we could file the pad lock off the gate, then go in and turn around, we would leave our own pad lock on the gate, so it will be locked again. We told him the plan. He reluctantly agreed, but let us know we would all be breaking the law.

Dana said, "I don't see where we have any other choice. We can't leave it here because it's blocking the intersection. We don't intend to steal anything, just turn around and relock the gate."

Ed said, "lets go!"

I went to the cab, picked up the flashlight and followed them. It was dusk so we might need the light.

Chapter 20

At the gate, we pulled the vines away from the lock. Ed started filing the lock, while Dana and I pulled all the vines and weeds off the whole gate so it would open once we had the pad lock off. Soon Ed was looking tired so I started filing.

I looked at the small indent he had put in the lock and thought this would take forever. Dana took a turn. We kept switching filers. The three of us were giggling and filing when a light shined on us. We suddenly stopped and looked into it, but couldn't see a thing.

We could see a tall figure with blue uniform on, who walked up to us and said, "What's going on here?" in a deep voice.

I jumped in to say, "Sir, Its not what it looks like. Dana and I were driving this truck to the instructions on the bill of laden. However, they were old instructions because they brought us down this road instead of the new one over there. I pointed to the right.

Dana joined in, "We cannot turn the corner, the street is to narrow. So we are filing this lock off, then we will go in and turn around, come back out and put our pad lock on the gate."

The cop said, "In all my years, I've never seen anything like this. Wait here a minute."

He walked to the police car, opened the trunk, and pulled out some tools. He found a big file that looked like it had never been used, and came over to the fence.

He said, "If you see another police car come let me know immediately."

He started filing the lock. It was obvious that his file was doing a much better job than ours, but we still had to take turns.

The lock finally broke off. We pulled it from the gate, opened the gate, and I went back to get the truck. I drove through the gate to a huge truck lot, turned the truck around in a circle, and came back through the gate. I went to the street passed the intersection, then stopped.

They put the new lock on and all four of us began to laugh.

The cop said, "This is a day I'll never forgot. Someday I'll tell my grand kids. I have one question for you, Ed. What did you use your wrecker for?"

Ed explained, "The trailer back axle was off the road and the trailer was tilting. I drove my wrecker down there on the grass and hooked it to the back axle of the trailer and tried to pull it back up on the road. What happened next was unbelievable, the trailer slide a little bit, then the wheels caught on the edge of the road and instead of sliding any more, my wrecker's front wheels went straight up in the air."

I've never seen a policeman laugh so hard in my life. It was time to say goodbye, and of course thank both Ed and the cop. We had discussed taking the key to the distributing office. If we take it to them we would have to tell them we broke into there lot. It would be best if we kept the key.

We climbed in and I drove to the main street, turned left and drove down to the correct entry street. I turned left onto it and drove to the end, where we parked for the night in front of the correct gate. Dana tied Bugsy out so we could walk across the street to a family restaurant, have dinner, and watch Bugsy in case the wild dogs came around.

Of course we talked and laughed about the episode we had just experienced. We both agreed that this day was the most fitting day for the finish of our first eastbound trip.

Back in the truck all three of us fell sound asleep. The sun was our alarm again, so we went over for breakfast.

When we came back the gate was opened. I climbed in to drive so Dana walked over to the dock, which wasn't far, to ask the manager where he wanted us to park?

He gave us a spot, which was easy just backing straight to the dock. They didn't ask us to unload the coffee, which is the correct way. Companies should either have their men unload or have men there we could hire to unload.

When we were all unloaded I pulled just outside the gate and parked. We knew phones where in the restaurant, so we could eat there and called the dispatcher.

Dana called the dispatcher and asked if we could please come to Los Angeles. Now the waiting and praying time was here. After an hour the dispatcher called back to say he has a load of rice for us to pickup in Mississippi and deliver to New York City Market.

"Oh Shit," I said, "I've never even driven a car in New York City."

Dana added, "I haven't either, you know what I think?"

I asked, "What?"

Dana said, "They are testing us. Trying to make us fail, by giving us a very difficult load and sending us in a direction we don't want to go."

"I agree and we are going to show them we can handle what ever they dish out," I said.

Dana said, "I wish I could be as sure as you are."

"The best thing to do is take it a step at a time," I added.

Dana said, "So lets look at the map to find the shortest way to Crystal Springs."

"Look here it's not very far, we have to take highway fifty-nine, which runs into twenty, and then runs into fifty-five, which is the highway Crystal Springs is on," I said.

We decided Dana would start driving, so I climbed in back for a rest.

After about two hours I heard Dana ask if I was awake?

I answered, "Yes, why?"

"Do you remember how high a bridge has

to be for us to fit under it," She asked?

"Yes, it must be eleven feet six inches," I answered.

She said, "Please come up here, cause we are headed toward a bridge that is eleven feet four inches."

"There are no short bridges on freeways?" I yelled.

"This isn't a freeway and there is a bridge!" I she back, "Look the sign says eleven feet four inches."

Dana said, "There is another road just before the bridge. I'll turn left on that road."

She had slowed way down as we weren't sure what we would do in this predicament. The new road solved our problem, however, but where did it lead?

"As soon as I can I'll stop, so we can find where we are on the map. Best of all, how to get out of here." Dana said

Fortunately, We soon came to a pullover. Obviously many people had made the same mistake we did.

I pulled out the maps and was trying to find where we were.

"It can't be that hard, let me see the maps." Dana said.

We discovered we had driven off our chosen path and were quit a distance from where we should be, according to our plans.

"Now what?" Dana said.

"Well look up here to the North. This is the road we should be on. Let's go up to this little road, turn left and we will run into the road we should be on.

Soon we were in the area of our pickup. I could feel we were on a bumpy road, now I was wide-awake. The road the dispatcher said to take, was actually a path, which looked like a driveway. Dana followed it along side a field. At the end of the field we turned right, from there we could see off in the distance two huge silos. Of course, it was winter. They would take the rice out of the silos.

There were three trucks in between the silos with no room to spare. Actually there was about one inch to spare.

Dana drove close to the trucks and parked. She climbed down from the cab and walked up on the dock. A short time later she came back to let me know we had quite a wait.

She said, "It takes about two or three hours to load a truck here. We can pull up to the dock when one trucks pulls out."

Being quite hungry we let the manager of the dock know, we were going back to the restaurant, we recently passed, to eat. The restaurant turned out to be almost empty of food. They did have eggs. Our breakfast was delicious. This was fine because we wanted to get back to the dock, so we wouldn't lose our place in line.

Back in line we waited about an hour. The middle truck started up and pulled enough forward so they could straighten theirs mirrors back out. The spot is so narrow they had to pull their mirrors in close to the truck for enough room to park.

Dana jumped down from the truck so she could make sure we could back in.

He said, "Yes, you can have the middle slot."

I don't understand why he added the middle slot because there isn't any other place to park. The truck moved out without incident. I tried to line our truck as even to the slot as I could. So maybe I could back straight in and be done with it.

No such luck, the space was so narrow, I had to stop and pull forward and start backing again. Just a minute turn of the wheel would through me off. I decided to watch Dana's instructions, this worked just fine. At the very end I had to pull my mirrors in close to the cab, also.

Dana walked upon the dock. She could see the manager inside our trailer with a flashlight, swishing it all around the whole inside of the trailer.

He came out of the trailer and said, "I have bad news for you. You can't pick-up this load with a hole in your trailer."

Dana said, "What are you talking about. I can see in there and I don't see any holes."

The manager walked back into the trailer and with his flashlight he pointed out the one-foot long scrap on the top of the trailer.

Dana said, "That's not a very big hole. Can't we just put some duck tape over it."

The manager said, "No think about it. Your driving down the road and a storm comes up. It rains on the tape comes lose and blows off. What does rice do when it is wet?"

"It swells up." Dana said with a chuckle.

"Just stay here for a bit. I'm going to call your dispatcher. I'll be back." He said.

After a short while he came back with an address on scrap paper. He gave it to Dana and explained it as the address of a business, which will solder a piece of metal over the hole.

Dana came to the front of the cab to tell me what was happening. She went out in front and directed me out of our slot.

Dana climbed in the cab, saw me laughing and said, "What's so funny?" "Can you visualize both sides of the trailer bulging out like a huge metal pumpkin, going down the road." I said.

We giggled for a short while. After which, we both were frustrated. It seemed like we would never be able to drive back to California. It was one problem after another, keeping us from our desired destination.

We read the address and directions the manager had given us and started driving to this business. From the note, it looked to be, about sixty-five miles away. I drove fast, but not over the speed limit.

I pulled along side a junkyard. I couldn't believe this, but it was the correct address. Dana went in and hunted for someone to direct us where to park. He was a tall thin unkempt person, wearing overalls. There was a partial building to the left.

He said, "Pull in here, turn to your right and go far enough so you can back into the building."

The ground was covered with pieces of junk. There were nails, sharp pieces of metal, and broken glass in the place he wanted us to park.

Dana said, "Don't you have someone who could sweep this junk out of the way so we won't get a flat tire?"

"No, it's too late, my workers have gone home." He said. "There are two brooms over there, if you would like to sweep it."

We each grabbed a broom because we couldn't get going unless the parking place was clean. It took about an hour. We had it so clean I could simply turn right go forward and back into the spot with no trouble at all.

Jumping down from the truck, I could see the boss was closing the gate and getting ready to leave.

Walking over to him I asked, "Aren't you soldering the piece of metal on now?"

He said, "No, It's too late I'll be back tomorrow to work on your truck."

"Well isn't this sweet?" Dana said, "How do you expect us to have dinner?"

The man said, "I forgot about dinner, go up the east corner of the fence and out that door.

Here is the key. Be sure you keep it locked."

The restaurant served mostly homemade food. We both enjoyed our dinner.

Back in the cab and in our sleeping positions, I began to chuckle.

Dana said, "What is it now?"

I said "I was thinking about last year at this time. We had warm beds and a shower. Here we are as dirty as could be and jammed into the small bed. Our we happy yet?"

"Actually yes," Dana said, "In everything we've experienced on this trip. I've laughed more, chuckled more, and cried happily more than any other time in my life."

"Thanks for straightening me out and good night." I said.

We both fell asleep.

Chapter 21

I woke to the noise of men chatting and laughing. I proceeded to dress and went out in the cab. I saw the tall man we talked to yesterday and asked when does this work start.

He said, "In about a half an hour."

I explained, "We will be going to breakfast, so the sooner you start working on it, the happier we will be."

Dana and I walked to the restaurant again. We ate quickly, because we wanted to pick up the rice and get out of here. The manager picked an experienced worker. He worked quickly and soon we were on our way.

I moved the truck out of this spot just the opposite of how I came in. I am beginning to feel quite confident about driving this truck and parking it. What a relieved feeling.

We backtracked to the rice silos. There was only one truck at the dock. The manager on the dock waved at us to park far to the left. I put it in there, but he wasn't satisfied. So again I backed in about an inch from the silo. He motioned perfect.

Dana went upon the dock for the loading. I filled out our logbooks and rested. I also worked out a route to New York City.

It seemed like forever for them to finish loading the trailer. These rice bags were a hundred pounds. Finally they were finished, and we could start driving. I asked Dana if she would drive because it would work with our schedule if she started driving. She put Bugsy in and then herself.

I pointed out the route and she agreed it was a fine one. I was happy about this because it put us on the highway our favorite truck stop was on.

The mountains were just as beautiful as the first time we drive this way. The trees were powered with snow. The roads had been cleaned off, since it snowed, so we could make good time. We were now driving the same speed as other trucks. Most trucks drove the speed limits, which we could also do now.

Arriving at our favorite truck stop, the next morning, we quickly tied out Bugsy and headed for the door. I felt of my hair, which was a little long for me, so I decided to have it cut in the big red leather barbers chair. The barber was free to cut it immediately. While I climbed in the chair, I could hear

Dana say, "Are you sure you want to do this?"

I answered, "Yes, I know he will cut it short, but think about it, when and where can we get our hair cut, out here on the road?"

With that I sat in the chair saying, "Will you go order our breakfast, while I have it cut?"

Dana said, "Yes, reluctantly," and left for the restaurant.

I felt like a queen sitting high in this chair. I knew, however, I would probably look more like a king when he finished. My hair was blond and wavy at the time. I knew it would grow to look different in two weeks. He handed me the mirror to check it out.

I said, "Wow, it's very short, but I like it and for the first time in a long time, it felt clean."

Walking into the restaurant was intimidating, especially hearing Dana's response, "You look like a young boy!"

"Can't you say something nicer?" I said.

She said, "It looks so clean and neat, I'd have mine down if we had time; maybe the next time we pass through here."

We ate our delicious breakfast. A clean and nice looking trucker sat across the isle from us.

He asked, "Where are you dropping?"

We both said, "New York City."

I added, "We've never dropped there before."

"Oh, my word." He said. "Would you like some suggestions with dropping in New York."

"Yes, we can use all the help we can get." Dana said.

"Well, the first thing is do not go into New York City during the day time. There are cars double-parked, red lights, and it is impossible to make your way through. You should drive in about three 0'clock in the morning. Now, no matter what happens, do not stop, not for a red light, not for someone in the street waving at you, not for anything at all. For if you do; you will loose your load."

We were beginning to feel scared, which he picked up on and began to tone it down a little.

He said, "You surely can make it, you just have to be careful and do what we are telling you. There are groups of men, who hang around late at night, who attempt to steal your load, by breaking the lock off when you are stopped. They jump in and throw as much out as they can. So again I stress do not stop for anything. I'll give you the streets to take, once you cross the bridge. Just stay on these streets, they will take you directly into the New York City market. Once you are in there, you will be pretty safe. The thing I don't understand is why would your company send you there without explaining this to you."

"I am not sure why they would send us to New York City without warning us first, but maybe they are taking bets on us making it safely." I said. "I'm just very glad we ran into you before attempting the big city. Somebody up there is watching over us, and we thank you for helping us out of a trap. We must be going now, hope to see you again some time or as the truckers say, catch you on the flip."

We left this truck stop again praising it and the kind of truckers it draws.

Driving North towards New York City, we were quiet. I suppose we were apprehensive about all we knew of New York City.

We stopped at a rest stop on the toll road, just before the exit to the Washington Bridge. This is where Leonard had directed us to stop and wait until three o' clock am.

This worked out fine because we now had some time to eat and rest.

The alarm woke us at two-thirty am. I dressed and decided to go buy some coffee. I asked Dana if she wanted some?

She said, "Yes and a breakfast roll."

I brought the food back, while she feed and walked Bugsy.

Once we finished eating I asked, "Should I or would you like to drive?"

She answered, "You may have the honors."

I climbed into the drivers seat and started the motor. Thankfully it purred like a kitten. On we went across the bridge. Coming off the other side of the bridge, I must make a right turn. There were a couple of guys mingling at the corner of the bridge. I made the turn as fast as I could, looked in the rear view mirror and saw them running towards the back of the truck with a padlock cutter in hand.

Dana said, "They are still coming so speed up if you can."

I did and we drove away from them. This street turned into residential area. Surely just as Leonard had warned, there were several cars double-parked. It was a tight squeeze, so I held onto the wheel tight and went straight through the narrow path. I nicked one slightly, but did not stop.

Dana said, "Even faster if you can."

I drove faster, however, I knew there was a left turn I would have too make soon. There was a red light I could see up ahead and thought I know I can't stop there. Coming up on the light, I could see the left turn would be easy, because of no cars parked on the street. Around the corner we went and could have driven straight into the market.

Dana said, "let's drive up to the next corner. There is someone standing there with a fur coat on."

There were no men running after us now so I said, "All right I want to see who that is, too."

As we came close to this character, she waved as over to us. I pulled up by the corner and could see she was a woman.

She reached down and flung her fur coat open, so I could see she was nude under it.

"Get out of here!" I heard Dana say, "She opened her coat because your hair cut makes you look mannish."

"Oh she would have opened her coat even if my hair was long." I said.

"Well, she is a prostitute, so pull up to the

driveway and into the market, quickly!" Dana said.

I followed her instructions as I was thinking the same thing. In the market I couldn't believe my eyes. Everything illegal and evil, you could think of, was happening in this unbelievable area of New York City. There was stealing, gambling, whores, drugs, and who knows what else.

I drove around to find the address for delivery. It was an easy back up, to the dock. Dana went to find the manager for this company. He looked at our bill of laden and told her we had to take this to the drops. Being new at this job, which he sensed, we didn't know he was scamming us. He was supposed to take the load from us, put it on little trucks, which could drive through places like Manhattan, easily.

Not knowing the unwritten rules of trucking, Dana pulled out the map, so we could find our way to Manhattan. We both thought we were doing the right thing.

The map showed Manhattan at the south end of this island. Again I asked if she would like to drive, pointing out the experience would be excellent for her.

She thought for a minute, and said, "I'm not confident enough yet, however, I know I will be soon."

The street for our delivery was luckily on our state map. I just had to take one street over to it. I was on my way. It was still early, so the traffic was bearable. Even with this traffic, the people here blow their horns for every little thing. I had to adapt to the horns because in Michigan we almost never blow our horns.

On we drove in New York City towards Manhattan. It was kind of like an obstacle race. Taxicabs went quickly from one spot to another, which meant you had to watch them every minute they were around you. I decided to drive slow and straight down the lane. This helped as the other drivers could predict where I was going.

The buildings were the tallest I've seen and they were taller the farther we went.

Dana said. "There is the address we are looking for."

I said, "It can't be, we can't deliver to skyscrapers! There's no dock. I'm going up around the next block so we can park in front and you can run in to talk to them."

"I can't go in there like this, I look like a truck

driver."

"We can't take the time for you to put on your gown and high heals. So when I reach the front, quickly jump out and go to their office. Remember, I'm out here with hundreds of cars honking and drivers yelling horrible things at me, so hurry!" I said.

The scene was just as I described, except for one policeman knocking on my door. I opened the window to hear, why are you parked here?

I explained to him why, so he asked for my papers. I gave them to him.

He said, "You are supposed to go to the distributer in the market."

I said, "We just came from there. They told us we must deliver this load in Manhattan, right here."

The policeman said, "They pulled one over on you. It is their job to take your load off to deliver it in small trucks. I'm sure you can understand why."

"Yes sir I can, but this is our first delivery in New York and we thought they were telling us the truth."

Just then Dana came running to the truck, saw the policeman and said, "We are moving right now. I'm sorry we made a mistake."

Dana said to me, "Go back to the market. We must deliver there."

It was much harder going back, so I drove as I had before. Holding the wheel tight, staying in my lane moving slowly. We soon were back at the market. I drove to the distributer's address we had on our papers. There was a police car parked by the dock. We saw the same policeman, who had talked to me in Manhattan, come off the dock get into his car and leave.

Dana walked up on the dock the manager came out, took one look at her and told us to parkway out in the front. She said the manager is furious. He said we have to wait until all the trucks are unloaded.

"There are no other trucks," I said.

"I know, but he is so angry, we will have to wait for a long time. He will come to let us know when we can be unloaded," Dana said.

I said, "See the pool of water out in front of the dock."

Dana said, "Good idea, park in the middle of it."

I said, "He is going to get his feet wet and that's nothing close to what he did to us."

We put ourselves in a comfortable position in the cab to wait. It took three and a half hours for him to finally come out to our truck. The puddle was huge, so there was no getting around the fact that he would have to walk through it. I pretended to be sleeping. The door and windows were closed because it was cold out. He had to walk through water up to his ankles, to knock on the door to let us know we could now back up to the dock.

The load was off in two hours. We backtracked to the rest area for dinner. This place also had phones, so Dana could call our dispatcher. I went with her because I was anxious to know if we could go back to Los Angeles.

Dana dialed and said, "Sir, please give us a load to Los Angeles." Some time went by while she was on hold.

Dana yelled, "Yes! Yes! Thank you very much."

I was jumping up and down, while waiting for her to get the address of our load. She hung up the phone and we both celebrated. We ate dinner and to make along story short, we delivered our load to Los Angeles, met up with Jake in San Diego, and received our new

Kenworth Truck. The truck was all we thought it would be.

My life, as you can see, was completely different from teaching. It was more physically difficult, very hard on our health, and an unconventional way for women in those days to earn a living. Our friends and relatives criticized us for changing occupations. However, We were both very happy, excited, and couldn't wait to see where we would go next trip.

> Catch you on the flip.
> Jill Shearer

Made in the USA
Lexington, KY
14 July 2011